The
GURU
Delivery

By Douglas Albert Boter

First Edition

The Guru Delivery
Copyright © 2012 by Douglas Albert Boter

Khrismattallie Publishing

Editing by: Ian Gibbs and Jeff Palley

Table of Contents

Chapter 1   An Unusual Hitchhiker   1

Chapter 2   The Decision   21

Chapter 3   Enlightenment Stew   44

Chapter 4   Proclamations   56

Chapter 5   Judgment Day   80

Chapter 6   Becoming Grateful for Coffee   90

Chapter 7   Room Service   99

Chapter 8   Shish KeRob   126

Chapter 9   Double Take   145

Chapter 10   Back to Work   158

Chapter 11   Clarity   178

Chapter 12   Saying Goodbye   188

Chapter 1

An Unusual Hitchhiker

I met him at a truck stop. I was instantly interested in him because he was wearing the garb of a Buddhist monk. Of course I was just as skeptical as I was curious, since he was obviously not Asian. Nonetheless, I figured he was interested in seeking things of a higher nature and that was right up my alley.

He said, "I can get you where you want to go."

"Huh?" I questioned. I figured he wanted something from me since he was approaching me, so I was a bit taken aback by his question.

He said again, "I can get you where you want to go."

I replied, "No thanks, I'm driving."

"I didn't say I would drive you there," he stated, "I said I could get you to where you want to go." I was puzzled, but he didn't say it as if he wanted something from me. In fact, he was picking up trash around the

1

fuel pumps and throwing it away. If he was wearing a uniform, you would have thought he worked there.

"And how do you know where I want to go?" I asked. I never liked it when somebody thought they knew more than I did about myself, and this guy obviously did. I mean how would he know more about what I'm doing than I do? He didn't answer, so I figured maybe he was a little off, and continued cleaning the windshield of my truck.

"So?" he questioned.

"So what?" I asked, slightly peeved that this guy wasn't going away.

"I said I can get you where you wanna go," he repeated.

"Yeah, I heard you quite clearly," I stated.

"So, are you willing to let me get you where you want to go?" This time the question was a bit different.

"No, now if you leave me be, I'll be on my way," I replied.

"Come on, you know you're curious."

I was curious, but a bit more perturbed than curious. Somehow I had to get rid of this guy. At this point I figured maybe if I just give him some money he'd leave and I was willing to give him five bucks just to be rid of him. As I pulled out a five from my wallet and started to hand it to him, he just chuckled and said, "My, we have much to learn, don't we? You're going to have to clear your passenger seat if I'm going to ride with you."

"You're not gonna ride with me," I let him know in no uncertain terms.

"I know you're a bit skeptical, but this is the way it works," he explained.

"The way what works?" I asked.

"The way the universe works," he said matter-of-factly. "You already know this or you would have dismissed me already."

"I thought I did, or at least I tried," I said. He laughed. He had a way about him that caused me to laugh as well. I didn't sense any selfish intent about him and my defenses were down a bit. I can be a bit naïve, and that doesn't fair well for a guy who finds himself in unfamiliar territory more often than not. For the most part, I try not to engage in conversation with strangers, which is completely against my nature, but it serves me well. He refused money, though, which was a first for me. I still had no intention of letting him ride with me anywhere. I finished pumping the fuel and noticed that he still didn't seem that interested in whether I would give him a ride or not. I took a minute to size him up and came to the conclusion that I could probably take him in a fight, and there was no way he could have been hiding a gun under that outfit. Still, giving him a ride had other disadvantages as well. What if he was crazy and I had to ditch him? What if he was a jerk? I mean, he already bugged me a little with that knowing where I want to go crap. Oh man, I'm already caving, I thought. It gets lonely on the road and having someone interesting to talk to sounded

3

appealing. Maybe I could get him to reveal more about himself with a little more conversation.

"That's how the universe works, huh?" I asked.

"Yes, there are no mistakes on the universe's part, only our interpretation," he said.

"I'm still trying to interpret you," I said.

"I know," he said with a warm smile. I was drawn to the guy. His speaking and mannerisms melted my defenses.

"You don't even know which way I'm going," I said.

"I can get you to where you want to be," he said again. "Where we go while you're getting there is irrelevant."

"So you just walk around aimlessly in life, with no place to go?" I asked.

"No, I have a place to go, I just don't know where it is yet," he said. He wasn't helping his case any in my mind, but I was still willing to give this a shot.

"All right, I guess you can ride with me for a while," I relented.

"Great, I'll clear the seat," he volunteered.

"What makes you think I'll let you ride up front?" I questioned.

"Seat belts," he said.

"Seat belts?" I asked.

"Yeah, I have to wear my seat belt," he stated matter-of-factly. "Don't you wear your seat belt?"

"Yeah, but I'm not begging for a ride," I explained.

"Make no mistake—I'm not begging for anything," he replied, smiling. "You are lucky to have me."

"Lucky me," I smiled sarcastically.

"Quick to get started learning, aren't we?" he asked.

"Okay, what do you mean by that?" I asked.

"Well, I'm glad you asked," he said as I was thinking maybe it was a mistake. "The reasons we do things are important. Even more important than what we do. When I wear my seat belt, it says to the universe that I want to continue living. Now we may not be consciously aware of such an implication, but that is what we do. Our actions are as important as our words. They tell the universe exactly what we want. I want to be safe, therefore I wear my seatbelt. When we do things with intent, we are more likely to get the result we're looking for."

Now he was speaking my language. It made me think that maybe this wasn't such a bad idea after all. And though he offered to clear the seat, I knew better how to arrange things, so I cleared it for him. After we got arranged and settled, I said, "And we're off."

"Where to?" he inquired.

"To a better place," I said with a big grin. He wasn't the only one that could give elusive replies.

"My name is Matt," he said.

"Khris," I said and shook his hand quickly between shifting gears.

"I see you have a refrigerator," he commented.

"Actually, it's an electrical cooler," I corrected.

"Electric cooler?" he questioned, studying it closely.

"Yeah, it's a cooler that does not require ice. It plugs into the cigarette lighter," I went on.

"Oh, so I was way off then," he said jokingly.

"It doesn't work on the same principle as a refrigerator," I replied.

"I'm just giving you a little trouble. I'm glad to see it, though. It will be quite useful," he said.

"It is quite useful. What do you mean by it will be quite useful?" I asked.

"On our travels I can prepare food. You also have something with which to cook?" he asked.

"On our travels? I'm not sure what your expectation is here, but I don't see this as a long-term thing." I explained.

"I can already tell it's going to take you a while. I can't seem to ask the simplest question without it being a long ordeal. So?" He dragged out the question while raising his eyebrows.

"So?" I questioned back, mockingly dragging it out also.

"So do you have some way to cook food in this truck?" he asked as if being patient with a child.

"Yes. I have a small oven and a propane grill. Though I have yet to be convinced that you will be with me long enough to use them," I said.

"Let's worry about that later. You'll find that I'm a very good cook. People are often good at what they really enjoy doing, and I really enjoy cooking. By the way, do you have a computer with Internet service?" he asked.

"This is starting to sound like you're asking about hotel amenities. Would you like to know where the pool is?" I asked.

"Very funny. I find the Internet to be a very useful tool to help people, in addition to being a great place to find recipes," he explained.

"Yes, I have a computer and no, I'm not comfortable enough with you to let you use it," I said.

"All in good time," he said. "So where are we going?"

"Now we're concerned about where we're going?" I chided.

"Not concerned, just curious," he answered.

"All in good time," I said. He was starting to seem pushy to me, so I was getting a little bit of an attitude.

"As you wish," he said. "You must come across a lot of beautiful scenery."

"Oh yeah, some of the countryside that I've seen has left me in awe of its beauty. Not just the scenery, either—the weather, the moonlight, the stars, the sunsets, the sunrises. They all make for some beautiful combinations. I've tried to take pictures, but they never give a real sense of the view. And then, of course, there are the bugs," I explained.

"The bugs?" he asked.

"Yeah, the bugs on the windshield make for a bad picture. I'm used to them and have learned to tune them out, but they don't make for a good picture," I said.

"Isn't that interesting?" he noted.

7

"What?" I asked.

"How you glossed over such a keen observation," he said.

"What are you talking about?" I asked.

"I see your observations about taking pictures through a windshield as a life lesson," he remarked.

"Oh? What do you mean?" I asked, eyebrows raised.

"It's easier to enjoy the beauty of life when we look past the bugs on our windshield," he said.

"Ah, very interesting," I replied. "That's the way I like to see it."

He was starting to speak my language. It was the reason I thought we might hit it off to begin with. You see, I considered myself a seeker of truth. Things spiritual in nature intrigued me. For a long time I read many books, from self-help and inspirational, to spiritual and religious. I think they created the new age section just for me. I practically lived there. For a long time I even yearned for someone to teach me, but had become quite discouraged, as I still hadn't found any answers, yet alone teachers. Eventually, I came to the conclusion that maybe no one had the answers.

I came across many other seekers during this time, and a few people who claimed to know the answers, though I didn't believe they did. I finally stopped reading and seeking, partially because I was discouraged, but mostly because it didn't seem helpful. Over and over again, I practiced affirmations, tips, tricks, meditations, prayers, as well as many other suggestions that simply did not work. My head was full of beliefs, but nothing I could prove to be true. There were many things I believed to be true in spite of the fact that I had not gotten results. I just assumed I was doing something wrong, which is why I prayed and hoped for a teacher. But alas, my belief that a teacher would appear in my life was not one that I held onto. I did, however, enjoy spending time with seekers, though not that many people seemed interested. It was for this reason that I had hoped my new friend would be someone with whom I could share my love of philosophy.

"I noticed you said that that's the way you like to see it. Is that the way you like to see it" he questioned, "or is that the way it is?"

"That's the way it is for me," I replied.

"So you can see past the bugs on your windshield?" he asked.

"I'd like to think I can," I said.

"I don't think you can," he replied, "but that is the reason I think I'm here."

"The reason you're here is because I'm giving you a ride," I said.

"Is it really? So you have no faith that the universe knows what it's doing and has brought us together for a reason other than you giving me a ride to nowhere?" he asked.

"How do you know the universe hasn't brought us together so that I can teach you something?" I asked.

"I'm certain you will teach me something, but I know that I'm here to help you," he said.

"And just how do you know that?" I asked. I had grown very skeptical after gaining little from self-proclaimed and so-called "experts," and had built a bit of a wall to keep out the BS. None of them had proven to be anything but a bit off.

"I've been doing this for a long time," he said.

"Doing what exactly?" I asked.

"Getting people where they want to go," he said with a warm smile. Again it melted my defenses and I smiled back at him, shaking my head. I still didn't believe that he was anything more than company while I was driving, but I could tell I was going to enjoy the company.

"You still don't even know where I'm taking you," I said with a grin. I felt a bit like I was trying to outwit him and was enjoying the competition. This was the most stimulating conversation I had had in a long time, and I was enjoying it.

"So, what's with the getup?" I asked.

"The getup?" he replied.

"Yeah, the whole bathrobe-and-tennis-shoes thing doesn't seem to be working for you," I chided.

"You have a thick head of curly hair, so you must be from a different cult than I'm used to seeing. The Hare Krishna types look like they're pooping out hair from the back of their head; the Buddhist monks shave their heads; some of the Native Americans as well as the hippie types do the ponytail; but not you man—thick, curly head of hair. Sooo, what gives?"

"That wasn't a list of cults, you know," he said as if a little offended.

"I know they're not, but I figure maybe you are and I'm not familiar with any that are bushy-haired. Granted, my experience with cults is limited. That Koresh fellow had a thick, curly head of hair, now didn't he? You know the fellow who stirred up all the trouble in Waco?" I laughed. "You know you kind of look like him? Well you don't have the glasses and you seem to smile a lot more. I'm guessing that you're not passing the torch along on that one, though."

He did have a thick head of curly hair, but he didn't really resemble David Koresh; I was just giving him trouble.

He smiled when I was having fun with him, but when I was done, he kind of sighed and replied, "Yeah, I haven't really figured out my look yet. I thought I would continue to wear the robe after I left the monastery—you know, as a way of keeping myself grounded and keeping things simple, but I let my hair grow out and found tennis shoes to be more practical for traveling. The look seems to be working against me, however."

"I'll say," I laughed. "Monastery?"

"Yes, my spiritual path led me to a Buddhist monastery. It was there that I found my spirituality," he proclaimed.

"You know you didn't have to go a Buddhist monastery to find your spirituality, right? Your spirituality is within," I explained, feeling a little cocky.

"I know that now, but I had to go to the Buddhist monastery to figure that out," he replied with a smile that let me know he was quite pleased with himself for figuring that out, even if it seemed like a simple concept to me. "We each have things in this life we are here to learn. That was one of my lessons. After I had learned it, I no longer needed to stay at the monastery. I knew I was best suited to help others in a more direct way. Also, I love to travel and so here we are."

"So you just randomly select truck drivers to ride with?" I asked.

"Oh, no," he corrected, "You're the first truck driver. I'd never been in a truck before today. I have to say, I really enjoy the view from up here."

"Then you'll really enjoy the view when we pass a car with nice seat covers. It's summertime, you know."

"Seat covers?" he questioned, and I could tell by the expression on his face that a moment after he said that, he realized that I was talking about pretty women driving by. "Oh yeah, seat covers. I hadn't thought of that."

"So your religion doesn't take issue with the appreciation of the female form?" I asked.

"Currently, I am without a religion to hang my hat on. For that matter, I am without a hat." He was nothing if not corny, which suited me just fine. "And I certainly have an appreciation of the female form, though I would never get caught gawking."

"So even though you were in a Buddhist monastery, you're not Buddhist?" I asked.

"No. Even while attending the monastery, I considered Buddhism more of a philosophy. I just wanted to be engulfed in it, you know, to find my spirituality," he explained.

"Well maybe it's about time to shed it altogether, at least the look, that is. Time to get out of the in-between. Besides, I can't be seen with you like that; I have a reputation to uphold," I said while making the motions of straightening a tie.

"I'm waiting for the universe to reveal its plan for my look. Maybe that's what you're here for," he then gave pause to look me over,"though I seriously doubt it." He pretended to be as serious as he could, looking straight ahead until we finally shared a good laugh at my expense.

We were passing through Amarillo, Texas, around dinnertime, so I thought I'd treat my new friend to a steak at a place famous for giving away a giant steak dinners if you can eat all of it. He was proving to be worth his weight as a traveling companion, and although I really like to eat at this place, I rarely do. I don't enjoy eating by myself, and now I not only had someone to eat with, but I also had an opportunity to introduce someone to a cool experience, something I really enjoy. So the truth is that I figured I was going to get as much out of this as he was.

"We're here," I said.

"This is your destination?" he asked.

"No, it's dinnertime," I explained. I was going to let him know where we were headed eventually, but for now I was enjoying messing with him too much. "I hope you're not a vegetarian," I said, and as I said the words I thought, Oh no, what if he is? I mean, he was a Buddhist monk. He must have sensed what I was thinking by my expression.

"Not at all, I enjoy a good steak," he stated. "What, you thought because of my background, I would be a vegan or something?"

"Well yeah, I mean, isn't that one of the cornerstones of Buddhism—sacred cow and all that?" I questioned.

"Maybe traditionally, but my belief is that all life is sacred, including plants," he explained. He saw the puzzled look on my face and continued. "Scientists have proven that plants react to stimuli. That means that even scientists, on some level, believe that plants have some sort of consciousness. That means that for you and I to live, something must die. Even the most austere practitioners of Buddhism pray for the insects that have to die in order for them to eat vegetables and grain. It is how this planet is set up—life depends on life. Whatever I am eating, I express gratitude for its sacrifice that I might eat. If something has to die in order for me to eat, I would just assume it to be a cow, because they are delicious. Let's eat, I'm starving." Then, once again, he shared a big smile with me. Though I was smiling back, I thought it a bit pretentious of him to act as if he was entitled to my paying for a steak dinner, but I didn't mind.

At the table he asked if I was going to take a stab at their free seventy-two-ounce steak dinner. They actually make a big to-do about it. Candidates line up at a table on a raised platform, so that onlookers can witness the whole affair. There's also a large timer in the background, because it has to be finished within an hour. "Not me," I answered.

"Why not?" he asked.

"Well, I might have been able to in my younger days and maybe using mind over matter, I could do it today, but I still wouldn't want to," I replied.

"Oh, and why not?" he asked.

"Well, the steak would be enjoyable at first, but at some point, it wouldn't be appealing anymore, because I would be full. At that point it would just become something I would dread doing, and I came here to enjoy my food for a price, not do work for free," I continued.

"Pity," he said.

"I suppose you have some way of enjoying every bit of life, and therefore feel sorry for me not being able to eat that great big steak?" I questioned. I had run across so-called spiritual people who constantly criticize others before, and I had my defenses up for this.

He laughed and said, "No, no. It's just a pity that I have to point out the lesson in what you just said during dinner. I thought we might get a break, but wisdom flows from your mouth like a spring."

"Oh?" I questioned. My defenses melted quickly with his compliments, even if I had no idea what he was talking about. "I am wise for not ordering a steak dinner, huh?"

"Yes, but because of your reasoning, many people spend a lot of time trying to obtain more than they need, and if they ever do actually obtain it, they find it a chore, rather than a delightful experience," he explained. "Life lessons seem to come easily to you."

I pondered his words for a moment. "I guess I never saw it like that," I said.

"It's what is meant by finding the answers within," he said.

I hardly had time to contemplate what he had said, when the waitress showed up with our salads. As I peppered my salad, I explained how I thought he was about to criticize me in the way that so many others had. I felt a bit ashamed about my prejudices and apologized for them.

"It's okay. Prejudging helps one live a less complicated life. You put pepper on your salad, did you not?" he asked.

"Yeah," I replied.

"Even before you tried it?" he clarified.

"Yeah," I replied.

"How did you know it didn't have enough pepper already?" he continued his line of questioning.

"Most places don't put a lot of pepper on their salads, and I've eaten here enough to know that they don't," I answered.

"Right, and that prejudice serves you well most of the time?" he asked.

"I haven't yet had a salad that's too peppery," I said.

"So, for the most part, your prejudice—in this regard—has served you well. Just consider me your far-too-peppery salad, and know that it doesn't take offense," he said with a big smile. "Like I said, you're always trying to learn." Just then, the steaks arrived and he playfully said, "Now can we please take a break long enough for us to eat our steaks?" I smiled and agreed. We sat quietly and ate our steaks. Actually, I was grateful for the time to think about what he had said. Maybe this guy can help me beyond my spiritual funk. I was certainly ready. On the other hand, I just picked up this stranger at a truck stop, wearing a robe and tennis shoes, who had no destination in mind. Hmmmmm. I had much to ponder.

Before we even finished eating, I asked, "How do you know all this stuff. I mean, really know?"

"Too much, too soon," he said. "You are like a starving man. I can only feed you so much information. For now, you have much to digest already. Eat. Sensory overload is a wasteful experience."

After we finished, the bill arrived and my new friend grabbed it. I thought this was a bit rude, since I was paying for supper and it seemed a bit like looking at the price tag on a gift. "I got this," he said. He reached into his sleeve and I heard a Velcro-type noise. He then produced a credit card and gave it to our waitress. He could see the puzzled expression on my face, which I'm sure he was getting accustomed to seeing by now. "What?"

"You know what," I replied.

"You don't think that I am a man of means?" he teased. "You're going to have to be a bit more open-minded if you're going to learn anything. Why do I always pick the slow kid in the class?" I would have been offended, but his smart-ass grin always gave him away.

"And I got stuck with a teacher who forgot to dress for class," I retorted. After sharing a laugh, we headed back to the truck.

Getting back on the road, my mind was whirling. This was beyond my experience. I've had a hitchhiker in my truck before, though it was rare. I even had a guy in my truck who claimed to be a traveling preacher. He seemed more like a religious homeless guy who enjoyed offending people by pushing his religion on them, but he claimed it to be a certified profession. But I'd never met a guy like this before. Usually, when I meet a guy who I seem to click with, we hit upon a topic, and like a skunk's behind staring me in the face, I realize just how different we actually are. This was just the opposite. This guy seemed loopy from the get-go and now I was starting to find it normal. Heck, I was drawn to the guy. None of what I understood to be social norms fit with this guy, yet I was accepting all of it. No, I was enjoying it all. Maybe this guy was more like me than I realized. I had no idea where this was going and then I realized that he still had no idea where we were going. I owed it to him to give him that, he'd definitely earned it. "Deerfield Beach, Florida," I said.

"Oh," he replied.

"Oh?" I said, clearly puzzled that he knew what I was talking about.

"I like Florida—looking forward to it," he said. "No more discussion tonight. You clearly have much to think about so I will meditate and enjoy the drive while you ponder. Tomorrow, you have a big decision to make and you'll want to be well-rested."

"A big decision?" I asked.

"Yeah, but I don't want to add any more to what's reeling in your head right now. Try to relax and just accept things for how they are. Often, we fear the unknown, but opportunities lurk in the unknown. This is the part where I'm supposed to tell you to be not afraid." He was grinning like a Cheshire cat again, which was beginning to seem like his trademark. "Deerfield Beach and tomorrow will come soon enough."

With that, he closed his eyes and that was just fine with me, because I didn't feel like talking anymore anyway. His smug attitude still rubbed me the wrong way a little. That whole knowing-more-than-I-did-about-myself irked me. I liked the guy, sure. I mean, he was great company, but he hadn't convinced me he was anything more than a clever guy with a few tricks up his sleeve. But the fact that he didn't fit in any category I had for people was odd. I would have figured out any other person by now. Maybe he was right. Maybe it was best to let go. As I did, I felt a relaxation pass over me, and I decided it was time for bed. We pulled into a truck stop.

"Bunking down for the night?" he asked.

"Well, it's not deluxe accommodations, but I have a double bunk and you can sleep on the top," I said. I was comfortable enough for him to stay in my truck overnight. Besides, being on the top bunk meant that I would feel any move he made. Because the cab of the truck sits on an airbag suspension on the frame of the truck, it has a tendency to move. The higher one is in the truck, the greater movement affects the motion of the whole cab. Therefore, I wouldn't have to sleep with one eye open to feel safe. I gave him the extra bedding that I keep in the truck and we bunked down for the night.

Chapter 2

The Decision

The next morning I awoke to someone opening the door of the truck. My fight-or-flight response immediately kicked in and I threw open the curtain, fists at the ready, only to be face-to-face with my new friend. I fell back into a sitting position in my bed and waited for my body to calm down.

"Coffee?" he said.

"Yeah…yeah…yeah," I mumbled.

"Sorry. Didn't mean to startle you," he apologized.

"That's all right, I'm just not used to having someone in the truck," I said. "How did you get out of the truck without waking me up?"

"It's all part of it," he said.

"All part of what?" I asked, taking a sip of my coffee.

"All part of your training," he replied.

"What training?" I asked, very puzzled by this statement.

"In getting you where you want to go, you need to train. It's a skill, I can't just tell you how. You have to train. When you come across a teacher such as myself, your senses overload and you must rest. You probably slept deeper than you're used to, that's all."

"Oh, that's all," I mocked.

"Today is the day you have to make the decision of whether you want me as a teacher. What I can teach you is of great value, but I cannot give it to you without your consent. No one can do anyone else's homework for them in life, and this is no exception. If you feel you don't want what I have to offer, I will move on to another student," he explained.

"Ahhh, so it's money you're after?" I said. "I'm not in the market for a teacher at this time. I wish you would have told me this earlier, I could have saved you the effort."

"Did I ask for any money" he questioned.

"No, but I've heard many a sales pitch my friend" I defended, "and they all contain the words value and offer"

He sighed, "No. I don't want any money. If you decide to become my student, you have to help at least one other person get to where they want to go. That is your only obligation," he continued.

"I'm not hitchhiking across the country in pajamas looking for someone to help," I said.

He laughed and said, "I know this is all new to you, but when the time is right, you'll know who to help and when to help them. It will not be a chore and it will come naturally. You have until tonight to decide, so anything you want to ask me about, you'll need to do it before then."

We got in our seats and I started driving. "Alright teach, what can you teach me exactly?" I asked, still very skeptical that he could teach me anything.

"All right, for starters I can teach you how to love yourself. Then I can teach you to find what it is exactly that you want from life. Then I can teach you how to get it. Hence, I can take you where you want to go," he answered.

"Ah, so how do you know I don't love myself, that I don't know what I want from life, and that I'm not doing it right now?" I asked.

"These things I know from experience. I can see it in your eyes, in your mannerisms, and in the way you present yourself. It's even more evident in what you say. Don't get me wrong, I can tell you are closer than most, but sometimes being close is more difficult than being at square one. I can tell that you've tried very, very hard to make that last hurdle, only to fall flat on your face. Yet you still hold hope with great faith. You're starting to become weary of trying only to be walking in place. How do you think it is that I know

23

that I am right?" Then he said again, "I'm telling you, I can get you where you want to be."

He was very serious in his tone. He wasn't joking around or being flippant. He really thought he could help me. And how did he know all of this stuff about me? Did he just describe the human condition and I was personalizing it? I don't know, but there was something about him that made me think that maybe he could help me. I was very reluctant to try again, having been let down so many times. "You might be able to say that about anyone and it would apply. Wouldn't it describe most of us?" I questioned.

"Maybe a lot, but I know it rings true for you," he replied.

"How do I know you can help?" I asked.

"Because I think you understand the basic principal of this being how the universe works. Things fall into place when you've asked them to and, of course, you are ready. I know you've asked long ago, but you must be ready or you wouldn't have run across me. I don't choose students, the universe does. I just recognize them when they've been brought to me. Apparently, you are supposed to be my latest victim," he said with a grin.

"So then it seems I don't have a choice in the matter," I replied with a chuckle.

"Yes, you do. We all have free will. We all create our own lives. We can choose anything we want at any given time. I only give you a deadline of nightfall, because you need to commit in order for me to benefit you, and you need to be certain you are ready. The path I will take you on will get you where you want to go, but it is not easy. You will have to retrain your thinking and people don't easily give that up," he said.

"That sounds a bit cultish," I said.

"If at any time you feel you are going against your own belief systems, you may bow out. I will not impose my beliefs on you, only help you to better understand your own," he assured. "And no, you don't have to shave your head and wear pajamas—so I have a question for you."

"Okay, shoot," I said.

"Do you have a computer I can use while we're driving?" he asked.

"You need the computer to help teach me things?" I asked.

"No, we don't start training until tomorrow, if you accept. You really need to think this over before you decide. Everything you do with intent brings about a result. If you choose to study with me, you will need to give your full intent. You can't just halfheartedly jump into this. You have to be certain. Otherwise, I'm just wasting our time," he said. "So?…"

"I'm not sure yet," I replied.

"You're not sure if you have a computer?" he kidded.

"Yeah, it's in my bag behind the seat. I'm afraid you'll have to get it yourself. I usually keep it on a table top that rests on the seat, but someone is preventing me from keeping it there," I replied. "What do you use a computer for exactly?"

"I use it for e-mail, banking, checking the stock market, finding recipes, and helping people," he said.

"So you are a man of means," I commented. "How do you help people?"

"I answer philosophical and relationship questions on an answer site. I'm surprised you didn't ask me about my finances," he said.

"I thought it would be rude," I replied. "I am curious, though."

"It's something we'll delve into when you are my student. It suffices to say that I won't be a burden to you financially on this trip. In fact, I may reward you by paying for a meal once in a while when you've done well. Like I said before, there's no charge for my services," he explained.

"When I am your student," I began, "no charge except pass it on, right?"

"That's it," he said. "And though you haven't decided yet, I can tell the odds are good."

"Well, I don't have much to lose, the way you tell it," I said.

"Oh yes you do," he replied quickly. "You have much to lose, but once you've lost it, you'll be glad you did. Think of it like dieting. You will be eating things you're not used to and exercising more. You will be very pleased with the results, but you will not necessarily enjoy the regimen at first. You will have to follow me blindly as well. I cannot discuss with you much of the reasoning behind what I will be having you do, because your mind will be too quick to dismiss it when results are not measurable. You'll be giving me control of your mind, just as you would be giving your body over to a trainer to build muscles. Most find it quite easy to give over control of their bodies to a professional, but when it comes to their way of thinking, they believe they know what's best. That is why I need you to commit. At times it will be difficult for you to understand the why behind what I'm having you do, and I'll need you to do it anyway. You're an intelligent guy, though. If I were having you do sick and twisted things, you'd kick me right out of this truck and never look back, right? You have nothing to fear, but it won't always be easy."

"You make it sound like a lot of work just to get me out of a spiritual funk," I said.

"It is a lot of work and I know you're capable of it. In fact, I'm sure you've already done much more work than you've had to in the past. You just weren't doing the right work to get the results you want. That's why the universe paired you with me. You've kind of given up lately, and I'm asking you to start working again—the right way. I'm telling you it won't be easy, but it will be worth it," he continued.

"How do I know that you're any different from any of the other so-called experts in the self-help field?" I asked. "Do you really know how much time and effort I put into doing the things they suggested, only to achieve little or no results at all?" Recognizing that I was starting to tear up, I quickly stopped thinking about it and regained my composure.

"That's the frustration that I can see plain as day on your face, even when you smile. I know it well. That's how I know I can help. There's a fundamental flaw in much of the information that's out there. I enjoy getting people past that. Much of what I teach has been around for thousands of years, but without fixing the flaws in one's line of logic, it's like giving next week's winning lottery numbers to a dog. I can fix your flawed logic."

"So deciding to accept you as my teacher is admitting that my logic is flawed, and that's why I have to take time to decide?" I questioned.

"In a manner of speaking, yes," he replied. "Your best thinking has gotten you where you are today. By no means does that belittle you. You are closer to where you want to be than you realize."

"No, I think I'm still about twelve hundred miles from Deerfield Beach," I joked.

"Like I was saying," he continued, as if once again dealing with a slow student. "In order to get to where you want to be, you're going to have to go where you haven't gone. Being in the dark and trusting me to guide you is a difficult thing. If I didn't trust the universe so completely myself, I would think you'd be a loon to do it. I mean, you barely know me—I'm a hitchhiker that doesn't care where he's going, I'm dressed in the garb of a different culture, etc. You must place an equal level of trust in the universe in order for this to work. This acceptance is the first step, and the first step needs to be given thought, so that you can show the universe that you are ready. Everything I will be doing will be about your growth, including this. I don't teach to inflate my ego." He paused for a moment and realized just how serious he was being, then added with a smile, "Besides, it wouldn't fit in the truck so I had to leave it behind."

With that, he got out my computer and after a little instruction, he was surfing the Web. I was surfing my thoughts. I went from going about my daily life to contemplating something different with a complete stranger as my guide. I really wanted this to be what I'd been looking for, but it sure wasn't like anything I thought it would be. Maybe what I'd been expecting wasn't what I should have been expecting. Maybe that's been the issue all along. Maybe what I'm looking for had presented itself to me in the past but I passed on it, not recognizing it as my answer. I realized then that I was going to give this a shot. At least I could ask questions if I didn't understand something. You can't do that with a book. And if nothing else, I will have learned one more person's perspective on life. It couldn't hurt, at least that I could tell, and there's great potential upside. Honestly, I would have probably gone along with it just to have the company. I mean, I liked the guy. So I had my answer. I didn't have to spend all day, but I was going to respect my new friend's wishes and wait till later. Besides, I didn't want to start training in anything today. I had to put miles behind me, and just then, I saw the "open" sign for the weigh station. "Get in the back," I said sternly.

"Why?" he questioned.

"We're coming up on a weigh station and I need you to get in the back. I'll explain later… Take the computer," I said while pushing the curtain open for him. I closed the curtain behind him and went through the scale house. When we got back on the highway, I opened the curtain and said,"You can come out now."

"What was that all about?" he asked.

"Technically, you're not allowed to be in the truck without a rider pass," I explained.

"A rider pass?" he questioned.

"Yeah, it's a form that a driver's company gives them that lets the Department of Transportation know that the company's aware that they have a rider and therefore said rider is insured," I continued.

"So no rider pass for me then?" he asked.

"Afraid not," I replied. "You won't exactly be on the books while riding with me. I don't have permission and can't obtain it. My company doesn't mind so much, but they will if it's an issue, so you'll need to get good at disappearing from time to time. You know, like when we come up on a weigh station."

"Do you have to go into every weigh station?" he asked.

"Only the ones that are open," I replied with a smile.

"How often are they closed?" he asked.

"Depends on the scale house, state policy, budget, stuff I'm not privy to, etc." I explained. "Generally drivers refer to them as chicken coops. There are a lot of terms that truckers use, but with the prevalence of cell phones, the CB just isn't as popular anymore, so the language is dying off. I find the CB so irritating that I no longer have one in my truck. Some people get on there just to intentionally offend others. And now that we can talk to whoever we want via cell phones, why bother trying to find someone decent on the radio? Modern technology has scored a lot of points with me on that front. Since I'm not the only person that feels that way, it's even harder to find someone decent to talk to, since most guys don't have their radios on if they have them. Things have changed a lot since I started driving. It used to be that when drivers passed one another, they'd wave to each other. In fact, I made a habit of smiling when I did it as a way to spread love in the world. I still do it to this day, though I'm largely ignored. As a courtesy, truck drivers used to flash their lights to let the drivers passing them know that they were clear to get back over. Then that driver would, in turn, flash their trailer lights to thank them. That's becoming a rarity as well, I'm afraid. I still do it, though I'm rarely thanked. These are habits that I got into in order to be loving to others, and so I will continue even if I'm alone. Wow, I guess that was more than you asked for, huh?"

"Yeah, but interesting nonetheless," he said. "So what happens if you don't go in?"

"I don't know exactly, but I've heard tell of fines around three thousand dollars. I guess it depends on the state. All I know is that it's not a good Idea. Drivers who have overweight loads generally take routes that avoid scales or time their trip to go by when they are closed. Sometimes the DOT gets sneaky and sets up portable scales in known avoidance routes. A lot of highways and interstates have scales that read gross vehicle weight, built into the road itself. Modern technology has kind of put a damper on the old outlaw truckers. Most of the trucks are governed at speeds of around 65–70 mph. That's due to the rise in fuel cost more than anything, though. A lot of the trucks have electronic logs in them now, too," I went on.

"Electronic logs?" he asked.

"Yes. A driver can legally only drive so many hours in a day and must log them in a book. The current rule is after eleven hours of driving, a ten-hour break is required. When I started, it was an eight-hour break after ten hours of driving. I like the ten-hour rule better, because you don't actually get to sleep eight hours when you take an eight-hour break," I explained.

"Why not?" he asked.

"Well, think about it. When you stop working, there may be a list of personal things you have to do. Maybe you need to eat dinner or breakfast, maybe take a shower, do laundry, etc. With an eight-hour break, you may only get five hours of sleep. But with a ten-hour break, you can easily get seven or eight. A lot companies expect you to hide the delay time in your break time as well—you know, from traffic delays to delays at the shippers and receivers. Many drivers resent the logbook as too much government regulation, but I think more than anything, it protects drivers from employers. The more a driver drives, the more money the company makes. Occasionally, though, the logbook works against you. If you follow it to the letter, it can flip your schedule to where you have to drive during the day in the beginning of the week, and all through the night by week's end. Also, there's the addition of the fourteen-hour rule, which states that fourteen hours after you start driving, you can no longer drive, even if you haven't yet driven eleven hours. This often keeps a driver from being able to nap. He may be tired and in need of one, but it means that he would have to sacrifice valuable drive time and his company may take issue with it. That's why I dread the idea of electronic logs. Sometimes legally and safely don't see eye to eye," I continued.

"Wow, I never really thought about all that," he said.

"Yeah, and recently regulation has gotten worse," I stated.

"Oh, how's that?" he asked.

"Well DOT has come up with a profile system for drivers and companies. It works on a point system and it makes the drivers more responsible for the condition of equipment," I explained.

"Isn't that a good thing?" he asked. I mean if you're responsible for the equipment, then you can make certain the roads are safe for everyone."

"In theory," I sighed. "If I were to be as picky about the equipment I drive as the DOT is, then not only would my time be spent waiting for the shop, which can take up to eight hours on a simple repair, depending on how busy they are, but my company would eventually fire me because I would be a thorn in their side. The rules basically make drivers responsible for a company's equipment. Now, don't get me wrong, I thoroughly inspect every truck and trailer I drive to ensure it's safe, but if there's one marker light out on the top of the trailer, I'm going to do the run and write up the trailer light when I get back. Meanwhile, I risk getting points assessed to my profile. Anyway, I don't want to talk about it anymore. It's just the more aggravating aspect of my job."

"Yeah, I can tell it's a touchy subject," he consoled.

"Well, the reality is that it doesn't really affect me that much. I just don't like the fact that my livelihood can be so easily threatened when I'm a safe driver. There aren't too many jobs in which you can be fined for going the extra mile." I laughed after I said it.

"So do you like driving a truck, I mean overall?" he asked.

"Well I enjoy driving and I enjoy the freedom it allows, but it gets old being gone all the time," I replied. "I work six days a week for just that one day off. In the office, they call it two days because

34

technically it's usually forty-eight hours, but if they had to work on Sunday through Friday, they wouldn't call it a five-day workweek. I've been doing this for over sixteen years. I guess I'm just burnt out. I'm ready for something else, but I have no idea what. I don't want to go from the frying pan into the fire, but lately the fire's not looking so bad. You say you can get me where I want to go, but I'm not sure I know exactly where that is. Do you?" I had started my rant with a very frustrated tone, but it ended a bit melancholy when I asked that, and I started to realize the sadness that he must have picked up on. I didn't even understand why I was so emotional all of a sudden. I felt a bit vulnerable.

"I said I can help you get there, but no, I don't know where there is. We all have it within us to find our bliss, but most of us let others who have had it taken from them take it from us. I enjoy helping others find it again. I can help you find it, but that requires your complete trust. You will not only have to place your trust in me, but once again in the universe. It is not an easy path, and not to be taken lightly. In addition to retraining your thinking, you will be required to face your fears, and that does not come easily," he said very calmly and seriously. "Today is a day of introspection. You need to look within and determine if you feel you are ready. I will be quiet so you can be with your thoughts until lunchtime. Besides, it's time to surf."

And with that, he busied himself with the computer. I had much to contemplate anyway. I think I understand why he didn't want an answer right away. If I would have answered then, it would have been a resounding yes. My emotions were taking over, and this had to be logically thought out. How did I know he had the answers? I mean, everything he said made sense, but how could I trust this guy I barely knew to lead me? Maybe I should just go with my gut instinct. My gut instinct was almost certain this guy could help me and equally afraid as well. What if I tried again and failed? What if I couldn't face my fears? Could I trust living life without a net? My mind was reeling and I could tell it was going to be a long day.

Lunchtime came and we stopped at one of my favorite burger places. It's my favorite for a number of reasons. They do have a very good burger, but I wouldn't say it's the best I've ever eaten (though it's pretty amazing). It's just that the food quality there is first-rate. The hamburgers taste like what you would make at home, with real meat and quality ingredients. They have crinkle-cut fries and real limeades, not the stuff made from an existing soda with limes added as an afterthought, plus they even have free refills on them. You'd think that the mini grocery store that is a part of it would have significantly higher prices than a normal grocery store, but often their prices are cheaper, and because they have their own dairy, many of the items are fresher. On top of all that, they have a hand-dipped ice cream case with a very large selection of flavors. Every time I go to one of their locations, I wonder how they can afford to sell such quality at prices cheaper than the leading (and awful) hamburger chain. In fact, the only drawback to this place is that their locations are only so far away from their dairy and not nationwide. I suppose it's for the best, though, because I might end up being larger than the chain itself if they were. My new friend had never been to one and I gave him the grand tour. We got our food and sat down. "So, can you give me the rundown of just how you're going to 'get me where I want to go'?" I asked.

"No," he said.

"Why not?" I asked.

"Because you would pick it apart with your logic and be able to dismiss it," he replied.

"If I can pick it apart with my logic, then how can it be what's best for me?" I asked.

"Your logic has gotten you where you are right now," he explained. "You are ready to go beyond that. It's not that you're not logical enough to get out on your own, it's just that you can't conceptualize it until you experience it. It's like one of those pictures you have to stare at until you see the image. Knowing the principle of how that picture works doesn't get you any closer to seeing the image. Someone has to explain to you that you need to stare into it for a while until it comes to you. I will be showing you where to stare. Wow, these are good burgers."

"I told you," I said with a smile. "I know I'm supposed to wait to show the universe I'm serious and all, but I feel like this has all happened for a reason, and I'm ready."

"I know," he said.

"You know?" I repeated, a bit taken aback. "That's not the reaction I was expecting from you," I said, slumping back into the booth, obviously disappointed.

"Things do happen for a reason, but only if you're living your life on purpose. You must have made a declaration to the universe to further your spiritual growth, or I would not be here. Many people believe that life happens to them and that everything happens for a reason, but the reality is that you have to declare your direction in order for it to be supported by the universe. You requested clarity, did you not?" he asked.

"Well yeah, but I did that a long time ago. I read many books, searching, and I learned many things, but I finally stopped because I wasn't finding what I was looking for. The things I learned only took me so far. Now you're telling me that you're the answer to my prayers, huh? I tell you, my skepticism level just rose," I said, a bit perturbed.

"That, my friend, is a perfect example of why I can't explain details to you about my methods of teaching. From this point on, you will have to follow my instruction without question. You still have until tonight to think about it, though. If you feel you're not ready, I understand. Remember, though, that people often dismiss the answers to their prayers because they don't meet their expectations," he explained. "It doesn't hurt my feelings any if I do not meet yours."

I paused for a second, taking it all in. He was right about it not meeting my expectations. I was disappointed, though, and decided to sulk while eating my burger. I think sometimes the best advice given in high school was when the coach told you to walk it off, and this was my way of walking it off. Maybe that's why I didn't graduate. It wasn't that I wasn't intelligent enough. In fact, I passed my GED with very high scores without studying and without finishing my sophomore year. I just had difficulty with reading and writing. I found it so laborious that I got discouraged. I can read very well aloud, but that's as fast as I can read in my head. In addition, my attention wanders, so quite often, I have to reread parts I've already read. I suspect that I may even be a bit dyslexic as well. If one of my teachers explained the material in class, I would get an A; if not, I failed. Maybe that's why I hadn't been able to further my own spiritual growth and now I had someone to teach me, someone I could ask questions of. I didn't know if this guy was the answer to my prayers or not, but I might be able to get more from him than I could a book, and I had to admit that what he said made sense. "I know," I said.

"You know what?" he asked.

"I just thought I'd answer for you," I said with a smug smile. "I'm again going to tell you that I'm ready in spite of what I just said, and then you're going to say that you know, so I'm saying it for you."

He looked up to the ceiling, holding his hands in the air and asked, "Why do you always send me the difficult ones?" He then looked me in the eyes and smiled. "Good, tonight we celebrate. We must stop at a superstore so that I can get the supplies I need."

"You need supplies to teach me?" I asked with a queried look on my face.

"No, I need supplies to cook with. Your portable oven is probably too small. We're going to have to get a slow cooker and food, of course." He seemed very excited.

"I don't know if we can fit a lot of stuff in the truck. Besides, I only have a small inverter," I said.

"Oh, and a cutting board and a knife, plasticware, ladle, paper plates, slow-cooker liners," he continued. "A slow cooker requires very low amperage. Your inverter should be fine."

"I have plasticware and paper plates. You seem rather excited about all this. By the way, why were you so insistent before that I wait till tonight for an answer, but now it's all good?" I asked.

"I recognize that you have finished wrestling with your logic to get to the place of letting go. Once our eyes have opened, we can see. You had to make the proclamation of intention, though. We could wait if you feel you need to hold on to the security blanket a bit longer," he explained. "And yes, I haven't cooked in a while, and I'm very excited about it. It also brings me joy to cook for those that appreciate it, and judging by the places you've taken me to eat and by your stature, I think we share a love of food."

"Hey! Did you just call me a fatty-fat-fat?" I said with a big grin, patting my belly. "It's hard to remain skinny, given my line of work, you know. Obesity is common amongst truck drivers due to lack of exercise, and long hours of road hypnotism leaves you exhausted." Although I wasn't obese, I was overweight, but kept in good humor about it. "All I want to do is veg out when I'm not sleeping. Occasionally, I'll go for a walk when I do get motivated enough, but usually I don't have time for it. You'll see. Even just riding in the truck, you'll feel it to a lesser extent."

"And that's the way it is, huh?" he asked.

"What do you mean?" I questioned.

"That's your reality and you're sticking to it," he said.

"That's the reality of it," I told him.

"Your reality will change," he said with a grin.

"You can't change reality," I said, a bit perturbed.

"One's reality changes all the time. When you were a kid, you probably thought that cookies and ice cream were the greatest foods in the world. That was your reality. Now it is different, isn't it?" he asked.

"That was because I didn't know any better. I didn't fully appreciate what else was out there. You learn as you grow," I explained. "And cookies and ice cream are pretty darn good, you know."

"That was your reality then. You have expanded your reality since, and I'm here to expand it further. Reality is personal. We accept certain ways of thinking in order to survive and live well with others, but reality is what we determine it is. A lot of what I will teach you is about letting go of old thought patterns that have trapped you and kept you stuck. Think of me as a reality tow truck here to get your rig out of the ditch. Quit spinning your wheels and let me help you," he said with a smirk that let me know how clever he thought he was.

I didn't agree with reality being pliable. I mean, sometimes it is what it is. But I figured that I didn't have to agree with everything he said in order to get some benefit from him. And I liked the idea of eating home-cooked food instead of fast-food junk, though a lot of that junk I liked. "We'll be near a superstore soon, so you may want to make a list," I said. "What's for supper?"

"Enlightenment stew," he said.

"Enlightenment stew?" I questioned.

"One of my former students named it," he explained. "There's a lesson involved that we will get into tonight."

"A lesson? I thought we weren't starting until tomorrow, or are we jumping right in since I made my intentions known to the universe and all ?" I asked.

"We start training tomorrow, but there is a bit of explanation or lesson, if you will, that you need to understand, at least on a basic level, so that your training will benefit you the most. It's one delicious lesson, if I do say so myself," he stated, clearly excited about the prospect of cooking.

"Well, I do like a good stew," I said. "But we don't have a lot of time, so make your list as efficiently as you can, so as not to waste time."

"Ten four, good buddy," he kidded.

"Oooh, don't say that," I said.

"Why?" he asked.

"Good buddy doesn't mean what it used to," I chuckled.

"What does it mean?" he asked.

"Let's just say it's a term for men who enjoy the company of other men," I explained.

"Ten four's still the same though, right?" he asked.

"Yeah, thank God," I said.

"You're welcome," he said, and shot me that smart-ass grin of his.

Chapter 3

Enlightenment Stew

We got to the store and I practically had to run to catch up to him. There are only a few stores that let you park an eighteen-wheeler in their parking lot, and superstores generally do. The drawback is that you have to park at the back of the lot. My new friend went straight for the produce section. Squeezing this and thumping that, I thought we'd never get out of that section, yet alone the store. He was a bit disappointed in the produce area, but was almost saddened by the meat selection. I reminded him that this was a superstore and by definition, a variety of items is plentiful; selection of specific ones, however, is not. "Since we're spending more time here than I had calculated on, get some things for a few more meals so we won't have to stop as much," I said. "Maybe some sandwich stuff, too, You know, stuff that can be made while driving." He did as I suggested, filling the cart up so much that it was hard to push. When we finally got to the counter, I told him that I'd pay for half, except for that slow cooker thing he bought and the utensils, cutting board, etc. I didn't mind paying for food, but I wasn't going to pay for his hobby. He agreed and left those to the side.

It must have taken twenty minutes to find a place for everything, rearrange the cooler, rearrange storage, etc. When we were done, I finally told him that he was going to have to prepare dinner while I was driving, because we had wasted his prep time in the store. He didn't take issue with that, even though he wouldn't be wearing his precious seat belt, doing the work in the back and all. He said that it was extenuating circumstances and that the universe understood his intent. I rolled my eyes at that as I started driving and he started cooking. "Eat this," he said as he tried to shove something in my mouth.

"No. What is that?" I replied, trying to move my mouth away and focus on driving at the same time.

"Consider it part of your training," he said. "You've got to start trusting me, you know."

I relented, and he put it in my mouth. "Eww, why did you do that?" My mouth was quickly filled with the taste of raw white onion, which I found most unpleasant, to say the least. "I'm hoping you thought that I would enjoy the taste of raw onion?"

"No, quite the opposite," he said.

"I thought you wanted me to trust you? That was awful! Why would you do that?" I said in complete disbelief. Every time I started to trust this guy, he would do something to make me question my sanity for even letting him in my truck. I almost felt betrayed, even if it was something petty in the scheme of things.

"I told you, it's part of your training," he repeated.

"Well, it's certainly a part I don't like," I said. "What, am I supposed to learn how to distrust people?" I only keep water in my truck so that I only drink water in my truck, and I was starting to regret this decision, because it wasn't getting rid of the taste. Luckily, I also carry gum within arm's reach.

"No, the lesson will be explained later," he said. "I'm sorry it was an unpleasant experience for you, but sometimes that is the best way to help someone truly understand. Besides, it wasn't that bad, you big baby. Onions are known to make grown men cry, but really?" he was grinning from ear to ear. "Would you like a tissue?"

And with those words I trusted him all over again. In fact, I felt silly for overreacting. "Yeah, I want a tissue!" I said in mock anger. Then I gave a shirking smile that let him know I felt a little silly for being angry.

He continued preparation of his stew, and I was falling in love with it as it was being prepared. The smells were filling the truck. I could tell he was really enjoying it, because he was humming the whole time. He was like a conductor conducting an orchestra, and his song was filling the air with a beautiful aroma. We had just eaten lunch a little while ago, but I was starting to get hungry. "When's dinner ready?" I joked.

"All in good time. You're always so eager to learn," he replied. "All right, I'll let you start a lesson that should keep you a little preoccupied. Name a color of car that you rarely see."

"I don't know…yellow?" I said.

"Are you asking me?" he asked. "This is about what your reality is, not mine. I will not judge your answers, there is no right or wrong."

"Yeah, yellow then. It's uncommon to see them, but I see them on occasion," I replied.

"Okay, I want you to see how many yellow cars there are out there. Try to find as many yellow cars as you can," he said.

"Really?" I said with all the sarcasm I could muster. I felt like he was dismissing me the way you would a child, sending me off to do some mundane task, masking it as an adventure so that he wouldn't be bothered anymore.

"You ever seen the movie The Karate Kid?" he asked.

"Yeah," I replied.

"Wax on…wax off," he said with his best Pat Morita impression.

"All right, all right," I relented. "Yellow cars, yellow cars, wherefore art thou yellow cars?"

He went back to his stew, and I went about searching for yellow cars. "I found one," I proclaimed.

"You don't need to notify me every time you find one," he explained patiently. He had a way of making me feel stupid, even though he wasn't trying to, which made it worse. Oh well, I thought, at least I have something to do. For the next couple hundred miles, all I did was look for yellow cars. My mind would wander every now and then as it always does when driving, but I kept on task for the most part. I wondered if maybe this was meditation training—you know, bring my mind back on task, that sort of thing. My new friend had finished cooking and joined me up front during this time, but we didn't speak. I enjoyed how driving a truck allowed me to daydream, and I hadn't done it since picking him up. Considering he seemed to enjoy it as well, not saying anything either, I chose not to break the silence.

"Well, we're here," I proclaimed. "Time to try out your mad cooking skills."

"I thought we would drive it all the way in, what gives? I mean, it's not that late," he questioned.

"Yeah, but Florida's not exactly a truck-friendly state," I told him.

"What do you mean by that?" he asked.

"Well, some states have plenty of truck parking and don't take issue if you find space in a parking lot or business. Others, especially in densely populated areas, have a lot of local ordinances and business policies that make it close to impossible for a truck to park. There are usually stiff fines and penalties involved if you pick the wrong place, but the worst is when you get woken up from a deep sleep, only to be told to get lost. Then after only a couple of hours of sleep, you have to search for a new spot where you won't be starting the process again in a couple more hours. Driving around in the middle of the night, tired, angry and without a clue as to where to go, because you're not from the area, is no fun. The alternative, our game plan, is not much fun either. You see, we have to be in Deerfield Beach at eight o'clock in the morning. We're three hours away, so you would think that we could leave at five a.m. to get there, right? Well, after you factor in an hour for rush-hour traffic and an hour for just-in-case purposes, we have to leave at three a.m., and therefore get up at about two forty-five in the morning. And just to add insult to injury, because parking in this state is in such high demand, the truck stops take advantage of this by charging for parking. So even though it's early enough that I will get my legal ten- hour break in, I will only get about four hours of sleep and pay for the privilege. Oh, I'll lay down at about ten tonight, but I'm used to going to bed later, so I probably won't fall asleep for an hour or so," I continued to explain, clearly expressing my frustration. "Often legally and safely don't see eye to eye in this business."

"Wow, I never thought about that," he said, quite sympathetically.

"Most people don't. In fact, often people in these areas are not only unsympathetic, but they have a disdain for truck drivers in general. Never mind that we're bringing them their life as they know it. We're just the great big vehicle getting in their way, slowly and noisily," I continued. "And then there are the truck drivers that make us look bad—leaving their garbage everywhere, throwing piss bottles out the window, driving aggressively. Often those guys are the ones that keep us out of areas we would be able to park in, because the owners don't want their lots trashed."

"So how do you deal with all of this?" he asked.

"I try to stay out of these areas," I said. "Most places aren't like this, so it's not an issue. It's the reason most drivers don't like to go to the East Coast. California is its own nightmare. I'll spare you the horrific details of that state's department of transportation. You know they consider a traffic violation a criminal act there? Some drivers tell their companies up front that they won't go to the East Coast or California. I'm a bit more flexible, but I would leave any company that sent me to those areas consistently."

"Well, maybe after my stew, you'll be able to relax enough to sleep," he said.

"Mmmm…stew." I said, doing my best Homer Simpson impression. "I am looking forward to that. Did it spill at all back there?" I asked. Most people don't realize just how bumpy big rigs are. They've come a long way, even since I started driving, but they can still make for a rough ride, especially for spillable items.

"Looks fine, I bought the slow cooker with the lid seal on it just for that reason," he answered. "Looks like it's ready, and it looks really good."

"It smells really good," I added. We got out the bowls and utensils and set everything up to eat. With the first bite, I burned my tongue. "Owee!"

"I told you it was hot," he said. He did tell me it was hot, but I was hungry and it smelled good. Besides, I did blow on it. "I haven't known you very long, but I've already assessed that you've got the patience of a flea."

"Well, this flea has the stomach of an ox, and if you keep feeding me like this, I'll have the figure of a cow," I responded. "I can see why you call this enlightenment stew," I chuckled. "It's amazing."

"Actually, that's not why. While it is delicious, if I say so myself," he said, straightening up tall and proud, "it's also a good way to explain the first lesson. The first thing we need to work on is releasing judgment. You see, judgment is one of the most destructive things in our lives. It wreaks havoc on our personal growth."

"I thought you said judgments were all good, you know, you being a 'far-too-peppery salad' and all," I commented.

"That's not the kind of judgment I'm referring to. We all make judgment calls about what we want in our lives and make prejudgments based on our experience to simplify things, but judging things as good and bad is an entirely different matter and is very destructive," he explained. "Let's take the pepper, for instance. You like pepper on your salad, right?"

"Yeah, you already know that," I replied.

"Right, you enjoy pepper" he went on. "Although, if you had never eaten pepper before and I gave you a bowl and told you to eat it like cereal, you would probably say that you do not like pepper. The measuring stick that you use to determine whether or not you like things is personal to you. It does not apply to the worthiness or value of something," he went on.

"Is that why you shoved an onion down my throat?" I asked, a bit peeved. "You could have just explained it, you know."

"You are such a baby. Lose the drama," he replied. "If I didn't think it would help, I wouldn't have done it. You need this drilled into your head, so yes, it was done for emphasis. When we are young, we try something like an onion and decide that we don't like anything with onions in it. We don't yet recognize that there might be a place in which we can appreciate them. Onions are neither good nor bad, they just are. We only decide what place they have in our lives."

"Yeah, that's just an onion. What about people? Aren't there some people who are just bad? Don't we have prisons full of them? I mean, there are people who would kill their own mother for a sandwich. What about them?" I argued.

"If you were to read in the paper that a man fell into a lion's cage and was eaten, you would not deem the lion to be bad, would you?" he asked.

"No, but that's different," I said. "Lions act on instinct. The lion might have felt threatened or hungry or whatever. The lion doesn't see it as being wrong. What would you do, let all the lions and criminals roam free just to save the world from judgment?"

"No," he said firmly, "just as you do not eat a bowl of pepper."

I scratched my head. "So a little criminal activity is okay?" I questioned, clearly puzzled.

He sighed and explained further, "You determine what is right and wrong for your life, you do not determine what is right and wrong. We as a people not wanting to be eaten have determined that the lion needs to be admired at a distance and kept from getting into the public, so that we are not made meals of. Criminals must be kept at bay so that we can be safe, but we do not judge them. They are just doing what they do, like the lions."

"So wait," I interjected, "you mean to tell me that we shouldn't judge bad people as bad?"

"I am saying you have to let go of your belief that something, or someone, in this case, is bad," he said.

"So you wouldn't even be willing to say a mass murderer is bad?" I snapped.

"Why do they always go to extremes?" he sighed. He took a second to compose himself, and then continued, "Wouldn't you agree that a mass murderer is a bit of a different animal—much like the lion?"

"But he's human," I said. "In that respect, he's nothing like a lion."

"You're right," he said, "more like a rabid dog."

"Uhhhhh, huh?" again I was scratching my head.

"He's obviously not well, right? We could discuss all of the possible reasons why, but the bottom line is that something's not right with his brain—you know, sick in the head?" he explained.

"Ohhh," I said. "So he's not responsible for his actions."

"No, he is responsible for his actions, which is why he's in prison, in addition to keeping the public safe, of course. He's not bad or good—he just is," he explained.

"Yeah, that's a tough pill to swallow," I replied.

"And you need to swallow it. Your growth depends on it," he said. "Tomorrow, we start working on it—tonight, you do."

"You're very confusing sometimes. Anyway, I have to go to bed early tonight, and I can't work on anything. I think your stew will help me with that," I yawned. "Tomorrow, I'll be up for it."

"When will you learn to trust me?" he asked.

"Look, I can't do it tonight; I have to get up too early.".

"Don't you think that I'm aware of that?" he asked.

"What...are you going to deprive me of sleep so that I'll accept what you have to say—defenses being lowered and all?" I asked. "I can't risk getting into an accident due to lack of sleep, not going to happen."

"Let me explain, before you lash out at me further. When you sleep, you can direct your dreams. The only work you need to do is in your sleep, so chill," he stated. "Before you go to sleep, I need you to ask yourself to be given a greater understanding in your dreams of what we discussed. That's it. Think you can handle that, sleepy head?"

I was starting to think that maybe it wasn't in my best interest to try to argue with this guy. Quite frankly and more specifically, I was tired of feeling stupid. "Yeah, I can do that," I responded sheepishly. I didn't think it would actually do any good, but I sure as heck wasn't going to question anything else he said tonight. Besides, I figured that it couldn't hurt, since any learning that would come to me in sleep couldn't be directed by him, so I could trust it. So I did, and as soon as my head hit the pillow, that wonderful stew sang me a lullaby that I couldn't refuse.

Chapter 4

Proclamations

The next morning I awoke to my alarm. I hate that. Most days I just sleep and wake up when I get up. Occasionally, I awake to someone banging on my door (also unpleasant), or a hard rain (hard rains are quite loud in a truck), but the most difficult way for me is the alarm. There are a few benefits driving a truck has over a more traditional job, and being allowed to wake up when I'm ready is one I cherish. "Time to get up," I announced. I heard some grumbling and the truck moved, so I knew he was stirring. I started getting things ready to go, which we needed to do quickly. The truck was still, and I didn't hear any rustling. I stood up and shook him a bit, saying that it was time to get up.

"Doesn't this suite have an extended checkout time?" he asked jokingly.

"Look, I understand if you're tired, not being used to a driver's schedule and all, so if you want to continue sleeping, you have to do so on the bottom bunk. The truck's designed with a restraining device for the lower bunk, but the upper bunk sways far too much for safe travel, so you'll have to get up even if you want to go back to sleep," I explained.

"All right, all right, I'll get up," he relented. I started driving as soon as he hit the seat. "Wow, what's the rush?"

"Rush hour," I replied. "Remember we discussed all this yesterday?"

"No," he replied, wiping his eyes.

"Yeah, you are tired, huh?" I said.

"Unlike you, the stew didn't do me in. I was up for a couple more hours," he explained.

"Oh," I said sarcastically, as if having a revelation, "can't run with the big dogs, eh?"

"I'm not sure what not being able to sleep has to do with 'running with the big dogs,'" he said.

I laughed and said that I was just giving him a hard time. "I know you're not familiar with this yet, but when you're out for many days in a row, sometimes you can be more tired than you realize and fall asleep easily when you're not expecting to be able to. That happened to me last night, and I was out like a light. Sometimes this phenomenon works in your favor, like it did for me. I'm good to go now. Heck, I won't even need coffee till we get out there, which is a very good thing."

"Why's that?" he asked.

"Two words for you, my friend…Cuban coffee," I answered.

"Cuban coffee?" he replied, clearly puzzled.

"Oh, ho, ho, ho, ho," I exclaimed. "You haven't woken up until you've had Cuban coffee. I don't know why, but I can't find it anywhere else in the country except around the Miami, Florida, area. I mean, besides the obvious answer that Cuban Americans prefer a tropical climate and therefore don't migrate far from there. Still, you would think that such an amazing drink would be exploited as much as any other cultural treasure from other regions of the world are here, even if it would have some sort of local influence to it that would spoil it for the people of that culture. Yes, my friend, you are in for a treat."

"Sounds like some … some … some …" he couldn't quite get it out until he finished yawning, "something I could use now," he said.

I yawned in reply. "Stop that. You're making me tired. Why don't you go back to sleep?"

"I don't want to be too far off from your schedule," he said.

"Why?" I asked.

"I'd like to engulf myself in this experience," he said. "It makes it easier for me to help a new student if I get in their world a bit."

"So it's sort of a personalized thing?" I asked.

"No, not really, it just helps sometimes in communicating the material. Parables are a powerful tool in getting across a point you're trying to make.

Many of the great teachers used them to bring about a greater understanding," he explained. "Parables need to be relatable. Besides, it is empowering to be engulfed in an experience."

"You're going to be trapped in this box with me for a while if you're going to get anything through this thick skull of mine, and it's a bit like living out of a large car, so I don't see that as much of an issue," I chuckled. "Truckers are kind of the modern cowboys, spoiled rotten, maybe, but living life on the trail, nonetheless. We get to see a lot of the country, but only from the highway. Sure, if you're so inclined, you can make an effort to get off the beaten path occasionally — you know, dropping your trailer somewhere, catching a cab, taking a train or bus, but it costs money to do those things and it costs time, which costs money. Then, of course, there's the worry factor."

"The 'worry factor'?" he said. "Oh, you mean like worrying about your truck and trailer while you're out and about?"

"Exactly," I agreed. "Being in unfamiliar territory, you have no idea whether your stuff is safe. Not only that, I'm sure there are those that are aware of the fact that drivers do just that and take advantage of the opportunity. It's kind of a losing proposition all the way around. In spite of it all, I have done it before. It's kind of cool to catch the bus to the beach and relax for a while. There's a superstore in Florida that will allow big trucks to park on their lot during the day, and it's only a couple of miles from the beach, on a bus route. If we get laid over, we could check it out, if you like."

"Only if you don't let me fall asleep on the beach," he said, laughing. "Otherwise, you'll be transporting a lobster in addition to your load. Right now, I feel like I could sleep all day."

"You'll get used to it," I responded. "Hazard of this line of work, I'm afraid. I wouldn't think any less of you if you went back to sleep, I know what it's like. You'll become acclimated soon enough, but maybe you should rest now, huh?"

"Yeah, maybe you're right," he relented while yawning. "We'd both probably be better off if I did, anyway."

"Remember, bottom bunk," I reminded, and with that, my new friend was quickly sawing logs.

Somehow, I managed to bump the dock without disturbing sleeping beauty, but that quickly changed when they started unloading us. "Welcome to the land of the living," I said.

"What? Is there an earthquake?" he said, clearly puzzled about how violently the truck was shaking. In his half-asleep state, he was a bit frightened, but given my calm demeanor, he could tell there was no need to panic.

After I stopped laughing I told him that they were just unloading the truck. "When they drive a two-thousand-pound forklift in and grab a two-thousand-pound pallet of material, it can be a bit unsettling," I said.

"Wow, I can't believe how hard I slept," he said, quite sincerely.

"It's all part of the process," I kidded. "This lifestyle takes getting used to, it's a lot harder than people think. Let me explain it a bit this way, when I was driving my car one time, I was accused of being a 'jerky driver.' When I asked what they were talking about, they started pointing out when I was doing it. On each occasion, I would explain my reaction, or pre-action, to the actions of all the other drivers on the road. For instance, I started explaining how I knew there was a driver about six car lengths behind us, who was driving really fast and starting to get over towards the right lanes, and by his actions I could tell that he would more than likely be cutting us off, and we had a car to the right of us driving a bit faster, so by the time he got there, he wouldn't be able to get over further. Therefore, the best plan of action was to immediately let off the accelerator, so that he would be able to slip in behind the car to our right and be out of our way. I did all of this without realizing I was doing it, until I was questioned. The end result was that, although I'm an extremely safe driver, it can be a bit 'jerky' at times. The point is that information is being constantly processed in my brain while I'm driving. Although I'm not consciously aware of it, I continually scan and deduce the possible actions and reactions of all of the other drivers around me. This is all, of course, in addition to the hypnotic effect of long-distance traveling. It's extremely exhausting. You are experiencing a mere fraction of that, but your mind and body have no tolerance for it yet. Don't worry, you'll get used to it. Until then, just consider it a form of jet lag."

"Got any of that coffee yet?" he asked. "I'm sure that would help."

"Nah, we'll have to get unloaded first," I answered. "I know a hardware store nearby we can park at for a while, near a place we can get some, though. They should be done with us here soon enough."

"Good, then I'll go over the first exercise with you. You will be doing proclamations all day today," he said.

"Proclamations, what's that?" I asked.

"It's a phrase you'll be repeating over and over again throughout the day," he replied.

"You mean affirmations?" I asked.

"No, you're not ready for affirmations yet. Affirmations only work when you already believe them to be true, you are simply affirming them. You cannot affirm something you do not already believe to be true. With proclamations you are proclaiming to the universe that you are accepting them as part of your reality. It is important to be specific with your intent when working with consciousness," he explained. "There is a very distinct difference, do you understand?"

"Yeah, I'm with you. That makes sense," I replied.

"In making proclamations, the direction of focus is placed outward, like you are speaking in front of an audience, rather than inward. When you say this proclamation, you need to direct your focus in such a manner. If it helps, you can picture yourself onstage, in front of a large audience of mass consciousness. Or you can picture yourself speaking in front of great masters. However you choose to picture it is up to you, as long as your intent is acceptance of this new reality," he explained further.

"Yeah, that makes sense," I said, almost excitedly. "Is that why affirmations never worked for me? I was going about it all wrong."

"Not entirely, but I suspect partially," he said. "We're going to have to trick your brain into accepting information that you haven't yet believed, in a manner that it won't suspect. We're sneaking past the guards, so to speak."

"Huh," I said as I sat back. He was starting to impress me. I was starting to think maybe he could help me. Maybe he did know something beyond what I had read. All I knew was that I had a new reason to get a little excited about my spiritual growth, something I hadn't felt in a long time. I was actually starting to look forward to this. "So, what's the proclamation?"

"You are perfect and beautiful and I love you unconditionally," he said very calmly, closing his eyes.

"Okay," I said, "I am perfect and beautiful and I love myself unconditionally."

"No," he corrected. "You are perfect and beautiful and I love you unconditionally."

"You are perfect and beautiful and I love you unconditionally? Isn't that a bit conceited?" I asked. "You know this seems a bit like you're trying to create a minion here, right? I'm not sure I'm comf—" He cut me off.

"It's not to be directed at me," he sighed. "Ever get tired of being wrong when you make negative assumptions? You do it a lot, you know."

"All right then, just who am I supposed to be saying this about?" I asked, a bit perturbed.

"Everyone," he answered.

"Everyone?" I asked.

"You repeat the things I say a lot, too. Doesn't that get tedious?" he stated, shooting me a warm smile.

"Obviously, I need clarity about this, why can't you just take the hint? It's a bit of a struggle to talk to you sometimes," I said.

"It's all about clarity. You need to start being more clear about your intentions," he replied. "Don't you remember last night's lesson? Okay, listen closely and I'll break it down for you. You need to repeat this proclamation about anyone you can think of, anyone you see, anyone you like, anyone you don't like, anyone at all, as often as you can remember to do it. And trust me, I'll be here to remind you if you become lax."

"You are perfect and beautiful and I love you unconditionally?" I repeated.

"Really? Are you asking me again?" he asked.

"No, no. You are perfect and beautiful and I love you unconditionally," I replied, and just for levity I added, "Is this going to be on the test?"

Just then, a man appeared with our bills and told us we were good to go. I thanked him and we left for the hardware store. After some to-do, I parked and went for coffee while my cohort got on the computer. As soon as I got back in the truck, he said, "You forgot the coffee," noticing I was only carrying a small paper bag. "I send you to do one simple task…," he said, frustratedly looking to the heavens for guidance.

"Relax, I got it," I said while pulling a very small container of liquid from the bag.

"I need more coffee than that," he proclaimed. "Didn't you get any for yourself?"

"Now who's jumping to conclusions?" I pointed out. "There's plenty here for both of us," I pulled some small thimble-sized plastic cups from the bag and proceeded to pour two of them full. "This will put hair on your chest, trust me. One shot of this is like drinking an energy drink." After downing those, we drank a couple more and I put the rest away.

"That was good," he said. "I do feel like I've had my morning coffee. Of course, I kind of miss having something to sip, but that was delightful."

"I know. It's good stuff. It's sweet, but not too sweet, not bitter, just really good. The reason there are extra cups is because it's customary to offer some to anyone who happens to be around. Actually, that's how I got my first taste," I explained.

"Well, I can see why you like it. Thank you for sharing the experience with me. And now I have something to share with you," he said while rustling around with his sleeves. He produced a small glass eyedropper bottle. "You need to put a few drops of this underneath your tongue."

I don't have a very good poker face at all, and my concern was well-expressed, but I was going to try and play it off as best I could, given that I was supposed to trust this guy. "Oh, is that all?" I said. "Just put something under my tongue from a guy I hardly know. My mom would be so proud. Look, I'm learning to trust you, but this requires a bit of explanation. In a few minutes I'm going to have to call my dispatcher, and I will have a real problem if the phone starts melting in my hand because I'm having some sort of 'spiritual experience.'"

"I actually have no problem with that; in fact, I would expect as much," he said. "This is actually an option, you can do all of the spiritual work without it. This is essentially the same thing Moses fed to his people after burning the gold statue they made. It is an ingestible form of gold. It has been broken down to a single element. What it is essentially is a superconductor. You've heard of the energy force inside you that Eastern medicine bases their healing techniques on?"

"Yeah, the chi, I think it's called," I replied.

"Yes, well essentially, it's electrical in nature. In fact, your chakras are electrical fields located around glands in the body. The ones we will be working on are located in the brain. This substance will better charge your entire system, so to speak, and make it easier for your lessons to sink in," he explained. "Although the version I'll be giving you is derived from gold, this substance is found in many places. At one time, we were able to get them naturally from our food. However, due to modern farming techniques, the soil we grow food on has very little. It can also be extracted from sea salt and from plain water. I actually prefer the water, but it is impractical to travel with, since one would need about a half gallon a week or so. The contraption that makes it is about the size of a basketball, so making it on the road is impractical as well, because, as you can see, I like to travel light. Just think of it as sort of a mineral supplement. You probably won't notice much of an effect at all, because it's very subtle and you're not very tuned in to your energy fields. Of course, if you took it at night, you would notice, because you wouldn't be able to slow your thoughts enough to sleep."

"I tell you what," I said, "I'll take it if you will." This guy had managed to impress me to the point that I trusted him almost completely in a very short period of time. "In keeping with the theme of non-judgment, I still recognize that there are many creatures in the wild that are very good at fooling their prey. I trust you enough to try this, but I'm playing on the side of caution as much as I can. You first."

"It only requires a few drops under the tongue," he said as he did it. He handed me the bottle.

"I'm just going to hang onto this for a while, till I see just how it affects you," I said, staring at him intently. He started laughing as much as he could, while keeping his mouth closed. Apparently, I amused him, so I decided to play into it. "I've got my eye on you," I said in jest, much like an authority figure would.

I called into dispatch and found out we were picking up at Winter Haven, Florida, tomorrow morning. It was only a hundred and ninety miles from where we were, so it was going to be an easy day. I expected as much because freight is slow coming out of Florida with a dry van trailer. If you have a refrigerated unit (or "reefer," as it's referred to), you can usually get orange-related products, but for everyone else it's a waiting game. Luckily, my company has this one run out here. Otherwise, we would probably be deadheading (driving with an empty trailer) all the way to Georgia, or waiting for a couple of days for a load out of Miami. "Well, we're in luck," I said. "We don't have to load far from here, so we have time to rest and relax. Make us some sandwiches?"

"Yeah, sure, meanwhile you can start your proclamations while we drive," he said.

"All right," I replied. "Just start randomly picking people, huh?"

"That's right," he replied, mildly frustrated of my constant need for reassurance. Heck, it was even getting on my nerves, now that he pointed it out. As we left the lot, there were a lot of people around the area, so I just started saying to myself, "You are perfect and beautiful and I love you unconditionally." I had to say it quickly to get as many people as I could in. I didn't want to leave anyone out, so I started saying, "You, you, you, you and you are perfect and beautiful and I love you unconditionally." I said it to as many different types of people as I could, and as often as I could. It's a long phrase to get out, so my mind was racing to get through it, and I was getting tongue-tied in my own head. I actually saw a very beautiful lady while I was saying it, and my pace slowed considerably. I was trying to let the words sink in at the same time. I was trying to see if I could wrap my head around this idea and make it stick. My mind started to wander and I wasn't repeating the phrase anymore.

"You aren't saying the proclamation," he stated.

How did he know I stopped? Could this guy read my thoughts? Maybe he was reading my facial expressions; he's proven good at that. I wasn't about to let him think I was impressed, though, so I said, "Sorry, I'll get back to it."

"Back to it?" he said, puzzled. "I haven't heard a peep out of you."

"I'm supposed to say them out loud?" I asked.

"Of course," he replied. "Anything you can do to give it more power helps. Saying things aloud is more powerful than thinking them. Singing something is more powerful than saying something."

"You want me to sing it?" I asked as if he were out of his mind.

"No. Saying it aloud will do, I did not sign up for being tortured," he replied, smiling. "In addition to helping with impact, I need to be able to hear your inner dialogue so that I can help you if need be."

"Won't it freak people out if I say that to them directly?" I said. I was thinking it might get me into a lot of trouble. "You better be a jujitsu master or something, too. Oooh…are you? Because that would be cool to learn."

"No," he replied. "You do not say it to anyone directly, or if anyone's around. The last thing you need right now is your mind telling you you're an idiot for doing this and have someone verify it for you. We are working on retraining your thought patterns. This is generally not understood by most people and will not be well received. Most people do not use the full potential of their brain and can feel very threatened by the idea that they could be using more, but choose not to."

"So you're going to show me how to use one hundred percent of my brain?" I asked, my face lighting up at the prospect.

"You will be able to use its full potential, but you will not have direct access," he replied.

"Why am I often more puzzled after you answer my questions? I think you're going to have to do it quick, just so I can keep up with you," I said.

"I did offer you something that would help this morning," he reminded me.

"Yeah, I figure if you're still alive and not acting weird or anything by the time we get to Winter Haven, I'll try your magic potion," I said.

"Till then, here's a sandwich," he said, handing one to me.

"Wait, what did you put in this?" I asked, raising an eyebrow and then laughing. "Mmm…is that apple I taste?"

"Yeah, good, huh?" he said, nodding a proud smile.

"I'll say. You are a good cook," I complimented. "Speaking of which, the place we're going does have truck parking nearby, but no place to eat. You up for making dinner?"

"Yeah, I could grill something," he said with excitement and then started looking around in the cooler. "Ham steak, potatoes and green beans sound good?"

"I'm starting to look forward to anything you make," I said, taking another delicious bite of my sandwich. I finished it off and started my proclamations again, this time aloud. After about three minutes of repeating my phrase, he chimed in.

"So when you're repeating this phrase, you're picturing an audience witnessing it, right?" he asked.

"Oh yeah, I kinda forgot about the whole audience thing. Thanks for reminding me," I replied and then continued repeating the phrase.

"So, as you're now picturing an audience, how do you see them?" he asked.

"I envision me being in a beautiful room on a raised floor in the center with spiritual masters all around," I said.

"Great job on setting the stage," he said.

"Thanks," I replied.

"One little thing, though," he explained, "You're picturing yourself standing in front of these great spiritual masters and speaking like you're writing sentences after school as a form of punishment."

"What do you mean?" I asked. "This is a repetitive exercise, isn't it?"

"Everything has meaning based on that which we grant it," he explained. "If you want this to be real for you, you need to convince your audience that you mean it. Proclamations, or affirmations, for that matter, need to be said with emphasis, like you mean it. They are repetitious by definition, but do not have to be the same." He could see the puzzled look on my face, which I'm sure he was used to seeing by now, so he continued. "Think of yourself as an actor standing in front of casting agents, and they want to see how diversely you can say a line and still bring its meaning across. You are perfect and beautiful and I love you unconditionally. You are perfect and beautiful and I love you unconditionally." Each time he said it, it was very different and equally compelling. I felt like a bit of a heel, doing it the way I was after hearing that.

"You are perfect and beautiful and I love you unconditionally," I said as if saying the most important thing I had ever said.

"Bravo!" he exclaimed. "You say proclamations like that and they'll be affirmations in no time." I bowed, well, as best as I could while driving. "Remember to visualize saying this to whichever person it's directed at, but in front of your audience. By the way, I like your audience."

"Why?" I asked, again with my puzzled look.

"You could have chosen your peers. That would have worked well, but you chose to hold yourself to a higher standard. I like that," he explained. "Now get back to work."

It was a long trip, having to repeat myself over and over again, but I was getting the hang of it. Sometimes, I would picture myself as a newscaster reporting the most important thing he could ever report. Other times, I would picture myself as if reading the last line of a story, the one that tied the whole story together, or as a great spiritual teacher speaking from the top of a mountain. I did whatever I could to keep the line from seeming mundane, and I did it while keeping my focus on the person I was saying it about. I had to take breaks, of course, and would sit in silence during that time. I found myself saying it to myself occasionally, though, by accident. I guess it was starting to become a habit. When we finally did get to where we were going, I was worn out. "I'm going to take a nap," I said.

He yawned and said, "That sounds good to me." We slept for about an hour. I think we were both spent.

"Well, I'm ready to try that stuff now," I said. "You seemed to have survived it, so I guess it's okay. I took out the bottle and shook it."

"Just about," he yawned, "a half an eyedropper under the tongue. Then keep it there for a few minutes. "That means you'll have to shut up for a while," he kidded.

"You're the one who's been having me rattle on all day, saying the same thing over and over," I reminded.

"I know. I'm just giving you a hard time. You've been doing quite well, I must say," he assured.

"Here goes nothing," I said as I started to measure out a half an eyedropper.

"Have you learned nothing?" he asked. "Buy him books and send him to school…"

"I'm too tired to figure out what I'm doing wrong now, could you just tell me so we can get this over with?" I begged.

"Intent, remember? Intent?" he replied.

"Okay, what's my intent?" I asked.

"Wisdom, unconditional love, understanding, maybe? I don't know, it's up to you, but 'here goes nothing'? Really?" he questioned.

"Hey, I just woke up too, you know," I said.

"For me I guess it would be patience, huh?" he said, realizing his own shortcomings.

I chuckled and then closed my eyes and asked for wisdom. I then put it under my tongue. It didn't have any taste, really, and I wondered if it may have been a placebo. I handed him the bottle and was silent for a while, holding it under my tongue. He got the grill out and figured out the best place to put it. I handed him a couple of collapsible chairs, and he started dinner preparations. After a while I started making muffled sounds and pointing to my mouth.

"Yeah, you can swallow it now," he said.

"Doesn't seem to taste bad," I said.

"No, not much of a taste to it, but it's powerful stuff," he explained.

"Uh, I thought you said it was subtle? This isn't going to make me freak out or anything, is it?" I asked.

"It is subtle," he replied, "subtle but powerful. Like I said, you probably won't notice the effects. You're not used to noticing changes in your energy. You might feel a little something, though. Over time you will notice a change in your awareness. You're in for a treat tonight. I'm making this delicious mustard sauce for the ham steak, and the potatoes I'm doing in olive oil with fresh garlic. You're going to love it."

For the next half hour I was taking inventory of how I was feeling. I didn't notice much of a change, but I think I felt something. Finishing his prep work with the food, he sat down next to me in the other collapsible chair and handed me a water. "Thanks," I said.

"You're welcome, but I got it for you because you need to drink plenty of water," he explained.

"What, that stuff dehydrates you?" I asked.

"No," he replied. "Your body is made up of mostly water, so in order to maximize your energy, you need to keep yourself well-hydrated. You're changing your way of thinking, so you want your energy levels to be as high as you can get them. Like I said, though, the stuff I gave you is an electrical superconductor so water does help. Well, so far today, we've been working on the easy people, people you don't know. Now we want to work on a few that you do. More specifically, people you don't like."

"I don't really have a long list there," I said.

"Really?" he said. "You seemed less than pleased with the law enforcement that deals with truck drivers."

"Well yeah, but no one in particular," I corrected.

"You don't have to be particular," he explained. "You can picture any highway patrolman with a hat, sunglasses and a uniform, just be vague with the features, okay?"

"Okay," I replied, closing my eyes. "Got it. Now what?" I asked.

"You know the line better than I do today," he reminded.

With my teeth clenched together and a look of disgust on my face, I managed, "You are perfect and beautiful and I love you unconditionally."

"Didn't sound too convincing to me," he said.

"Well what do you expect?" I snapped.

"Remember, you're acting as if, like an actor onstage. Convince me and the rest of your audience. You were doing so well earlier," he complimented.

"I just became an actor this morning and already I'm expected to do the difficult parts? I'll be in my trailer," I joked, turning my head.

"You can do this. It's very important to release all resentment so that you can be the most helpful to others," he explained.

"All right, all right," I said, and was immediately interrupted.

"You say that phrase a lot too. This could go a lot faster if you'd just relent more quickly," he said, smiling big.

"Smart-ass," I said and quickly followed with, "and if you reply 'dumb-ass,' I'll kick your ass."

"You better not try, I know jujitsu, remember?" he replied.

"I guess we're having corn with dinner tonight. Please, when will it end?" I said, looking to the skies. I took a moment and once again said the line with all the grace and poise I could muster. Rather than picturing a single officer, though, I focused on addressing an entire audience of them. I figured that since I perceive the whole issue to be an unjust situation, rather than a matter individual in nature, it would be better to broaden the scope. I didn't run that by the teacher, though; we had gotten sidetracked enough and I didn't want to continue testing his patience. On stage with me, of course, were my enlightened teachers to witness it all.

"Very good," he praised. "Now that wasn't so bad, was it?"

"Wasn't my favorite," I replied.

"You've had enough for today," he said as he walked to the grill to tend to dinner. "You have the hang of it now. Tomorrow you start saying it to yourself. This will allow you to think of people and circumstances that you don't like but would like to keep personal, as well as the random people you've been saying it about. I need to know that you are remembering to do it throughout the day, though, so a simple nod to me every now and then will suffice. You have proven to be very thirsty to learn. I am very impressed with you thus far. At this rate, it should only take a couple more days before you're ready for the next lesson. It takes a bit longer for most people because they do not have as much time to devote to it as you. Your profession works in your favor in this regard. I think you will get a kick out of the next lesson because it has a very unique way of helping your brain absorb the material."

I was only halfway listening. Four hours of saying the same thing over and over again wore my brain out. Besides, I was distracted by the wonderful smells coming from the grill. He was proving himself a master chef more than anything. I did pick out the compliment, though, and felt good about that. I was also enjoying relaxing outside. I rarely did stuff like this. Oh, I carried a grill and chairs in the truck with me, but I only used them when I ran into other drivers that I knew on the road, which was maybe two or three times a year. I guess hanging out with my new friend reminded me of how lonely it gets on the road. You get used to it. A man can get used to anything, I guess, but hanging out with someone of similar interest was reminding me just how lonely the life I have is. Normally, I would be sitting in the truck right now, watching a movie on the computer, or something similar, just to forget I was alone for a while. I certainly wouldn't be making dinner or sitting outside enjoying the air. I'm quite capable of making dinner, but it's hard to get motivated to that just for oneself. As far as sitting outside is concerned, I would be far too self-conscious to do that. I would imagine people saying, "What's that guy doing out there?" It wouldn't be the same without someone to share it with anyway. But now I was tired, comfortable and most importantly, not lonely, so I decided to enjoy it. In fact, we both sat in silence, relaxing after we ate his fantastic meal—the mustard sauce he made with brown sugar and crushed red pepper was really good. He said something about how he usually uses horseradish with it, instead of red pepper, but fresh horseradish was a bit impractical for the road. I didn't mind, though, I couldn't imagine it could have been any better than it was. Didn't take long before our yawns were leading us to our pillows and I was out.

Chapter 5

Judgment Day

They loaded us quickly at the shipper, a bit unusual for this particular shipper, but I wasn't complaining. We were St. Louis–bound in no time. My new friend nodded to me. I looked at him, puzzled. He did it again. "What?" I asked.

"Remember, your proclamations?" he said.

"Oh yeah. We gotta start that before coffee? Talk about unfair," I answered.

"Oh that reminds me, are we getting more of that Cuban coffee?" he asked.

"I've created another Cuban coffee addict," I said, laughing. "No, I haven't been able to find it up this far north. Pretty good stuff though, huh?"

"Yeah," he replied. I could hear the disappointment in his voice. "At any rate, it's time to start the affirmations."

"All right," I relented. "You are perfect and beautiful and I love you unconditionally," I said with all the enthusiasm of a teenager doing something they're less than thrilled about.

"Lost all your training overnight, huh? We're doing it silently today and with feeling, remember? I'm going to nod occasionally if you don't nod to me first, to make sure you're remembering to do it, since I won't be able to hear it. Your goal is to remember to do it enough that I won't be nodding."

"As you wish," I relented once again, though this time I wasn't as childish about it.

"And count this time," he added.

"Count?" I said, puzzled. "You want me to count the number of times I say the affirmation?"

"Proclamation," he corrected. "No, I want you to count the number of yellow cars. Coffee's on me if you can do it."

"Oh, okay. That seems more reasonable. Not near as many of those as there are affir—" I corrected midstream, "proclamations." I again started a regimen of the phrase about the passersby in traffic. I was getting good at saying it many different ways, partially due to practice, but not being listened to allowed me the freedom to be a bit more serious at times, and way sillier as well. I was just thinking about that when an absolutely gorgeous woman drove by. Without thinking I just stared and said aloud, "You are perfect and beautiful."

This caught Matt's attention and he laughed. "And let me guess, you love her unconditionally."

I laughed too and said, "I don't know about all that. We haven't even had a first kiss yet, but I'll let you know.

After that, whenever I saw a pretty girl, I said it. He actually started doing it too. I spent most of the morning saying the proclamation, nodding occasionally and taking breaks allowing my mind to wander, all the while looking for yellow cars. Finally he piped up, "We are going to get coffee, aren't we?"

"Oh yeah, I've been so busy, I kind of forgot," I replied. "Sorry. I could go for some myself," I said, yawning, now that I realized how long I had gone without it. We stopped in one of the convenience store–type truck stops. It was kind of the format that truck stops were turning into. They're no longer building as many truck stops with driver's lounges, TV rooms and sit-down restaurants. No, they're more like gas stations with fast-food joints attached to them. This suited me just fine because my entertainment was in the truck via the computer. Sit-down restaurants often take too long and the food quality of the fast-food places has gone up over the years. You could get a decent salad, for instance, at nearly all of them. But the best part is the coffee. I like dark-roast coffee made strong and cut with milk. I usually had to buy my own milk, but I love the variety of coffees available these days. Actually, that's not true. I simply like the fact that they offer a dark-roast coffee; they could get rid of the rest, for all I care. Anyway, I don't think they're designing truck stops, or travel centers as they're now called, less truck driver–friendly, as some of the old timers see it. I think they're just catering to the new generation of truck drivers, like myself. I guess I'm not so new anymore, having done this for the past sixteen years. It was then that I found myself spacing out, staring into the eyes of a beautiful woman, only to hear the uproarious laughter of my new friend standing next to me, as I realized what I had done. I had just said out loud to a woman standing in front of me that she was perfect and beautiful. I was horrified. I must have turned a shade of red comparable to a tomato. I decided just to flee and made a beeline for the register.

I was too petrified to look anywhere other than straight ahead when I felt someone tap my arm. When I turned to look, the woman I had run from handed me a folded piece of paper.

I was trying to think of something witty to say in reply to save a little face in this extremely embarrassing situation, but before I could get anything out, I heard, "Sir," the man at the counter was trying to get my attention. I put my coffee on the counter and reached for my wallet. By the time I paid for it and turned back around, she was gone. I unfolded the paper. It read, "You're not so bad yourself."

Here I had been trying to save face with her and she had handed me a way to save face with Matt. I was all prepared to show it off, but for some reason I decided not to. I just tucked the note away in my pocket.

We started driving again, and I was happy to sip my coffee and just relax—I was still looking for yellow cars. Matt seemed to have forgotten that he would be buying the coffee if I had a yellow car count, which was just as well because I don't remember seeing one. The rest of my homework got put on hold while I played the scenario of her handing me the note and my reading it in a loop. I still nodded occasionally, but after a while of that, I started feeling guilty, so it was back to business as usual. I did not, however, say it aloud anymore when I saw a pretty woman. I thought instead that I would make that my cue to nod. I don't know if he picked up on it or not, though, because he started surfing the Web on my computer. I thought it a bit odd that he would enjoy it so much. I don't know what I expected of him, really, maybe just to do a lot of meditating. He didn't meet my expectations of a spiritual master, that's for sure. "Here, I almost forgot," he said, handing me the bottle of that mysterious solution that didn't seem to do anything.

"I don't think that stuff does anything," I said. "If it's a placebo, I would just as soon not take it."

"It's not a placebo," he said very sternly. "And as I said, it's optional. At a hundred dollars a bottle, it wouldn't hurt my feelings any if you passed. I do what I do for your benefit, not my own. Every direction I give you is to further you on your own path. It is what I love to do. My pleasure is derived from helping others, and I am very good at what I do. People are usually very good at what they enjoy doing."

"Yeah, you mentioned that before."

"Yes, I repeat myself when it seems you have not yet gotten the point. However, I think I agree with you that I do it a bit much," he said, smiling brightly.

"You are perfect and beautiful and I love you unconditionally," I said sarcastically, returning the smile. "I guess if you're as good a teacher as you are a cook, I'll happily take my medicine," and I did.

Miles and miles and miles of that phrase running through my head was starting to wear on me again, and I was getting a bit tired. I pulled into a rest area. "Why are we pulling in here?" he asked.

"I need a nap," I replied. "This repetitive practice is making me sleepy. One of the benefits of my job is that I can sleep whenever I want as long as I make the load on time and make it look legal in my logbook, of course. I usually sleep less than an hour when I nap, so if you're not tired, I won't be long."

"Oh, I'm tired, all right. I don't know how you do this all the time, it really wears you out, huh?" he asked.

"Didn't I already explain that? Man, you're a slow learner," I chided.

"Touché and goodnight, my friend," he replied.

"Goodnight," I said.

Two more days of constantly repeating that phrase and I was to the point at which I believed every word. I was starting to see the beauty in all people, the perfection in everyone and everything, and my heart was growing more loving for it all. I was even seeing the reasons for people's bad behavior as that of irrational instincts, much like a mistreated animal, rather than them just being bad people. I finally understood what he was trying to show me and it was humbling. I meekly said to him, "I get it."

"Good, now we can move on to the next lesson," he replied.

"Really?" I asked, puzzled by his reaction. "No test? You don't want to be sure? You don't want me to express myself further? How do you even know what I'm talking about?"

"I told you, I'm good at what I do," he repeated. "I know you've changed, I can see it in your eyes, just as I could spot the sorrow that was there before. Perhaps we can move on to the next lesson now?"

I was hoping for more feedback than that. I had had what I considered to be a spiritual awakening and he seemed less than impressed. I was dumbfounded. "I guess so," I managed.

"Good, we have to do this one before you start driving anyway," he went on to explain. "Your new phrase is, 'I am perfect and beautiful and I love myself.'"

"Really?" I asked. In that moment I completely lost hope in this guy. I explained to him how affirmations like that never worked for me. Had he just ignored what I told him doesn't work for me because he's convinced his system works for everyone? Damn! My heart sank. I thought, Another false hope, another person I thought knew the answers, only to find out he has some stupid system that's just like all the rest. If a system out there worked, I would have found it. I have been through this too many times. Damn! Just when I thought I was starting to make progress and this guy had something more than the self-help, motivational section of the bookstore, I was back to square one. I was pissed. I hid my disappointment as best I could, though, because I still really liked this guy, and the last thing I wanted to do was hurt his feelings.

I knew he could see right through me, though, because he put his hand on my shoulder and said, "Trust me."

His words meant as much to me right then as the salesmen's words on those "As Seen On TV" products, but I said the words anyway. "I am perfect and beautiful and I love myself," I said, feeling kind of strange when I did it.

"Again," he instructed.

"I am perfect and beautiful and I love myself," I repeated, tears welling up in my eyes.

"Again," he repeated softly.

"I am per—" I could hardly get the words out, "—fect and beautiful and," I stammered, "and, I love myself unconditionally," I started crying and laughing at the same time as I came to the realization that I believed those words. For the first time in my life, I believed those words. "But how?" I managed between blubbering.

"I told you. We had to trick your brain into believing it," he replied, smiling a caring smile.

"I thought that's why we were doing 'proclamations,'" I said, sniffling and gesturing quotations, "instead of 'affirmations.'"

"As I told you, affirmations only work if you believe what you're affirming. You can't affirm something you do not already believe to be true on some level. Your mind could not accept the proclamation I gave you about yourself, but you could wrap your head around it enough to believe it about other people," he explained. "Psychologically, everyone thinks that they are the average person. So, essentially, the only way you could see the perfection and beauty in yourself was to see it in others. Things often work the opposite of what people chant. How many times have you heard that you have to love yourself before you can love others? Sometimes I wonder if the key to life is found in doing the opposite of what the masses advise. Now you understand exactly why judgment is so destructive. When you judge others, you judge yourself ten times as harshly. The less you think of others, the less you think of yourself. Likewise, the opposite is true. All I did was help pull you out of that vicious cycle you were in."

"All you did?" I said as another tear rolled down my cheek.

"I know, I know," he said. "It's a big realization for you. Just give it some time. You'll be back to questioning my tactics again in no time." Again, he had me laughing through my tears. I must have been a sight. My confidence in him had not only been regained, but strengthened. I couldn't believe what happened. I quickly shook it off, though.

"So what's next?" I asked. I was ready for more of this. I was ready to climb the mountain. I was ready to take on the world. I wanted to do anything to get more of what he was offering me.

"Nothing," he replied calmly.

"Nothing?" I questioned, completely puzzled. I thought for a moment that this could be it. "Is that it? I'm done?"

He laughed. "That's funny. No, no, you have much to learn, but today you must let it sink in," he replied. "Tomorrow, we will start solidifying this lesson as well as start a new habit."

"Solidify?"

"I know I've increased your thirst for more, now that you have tasted a bit of how life could be, but you have to stop for a while and absorb what has changed within you. You have the day off to reflect a bit. You need to start the process of understanding the lesson, so that tomorrow we can burn it into your consciousness," he said. Noticing I was about to say something, he added, "No more questions—reflection." And with that, we were quiet for a while.

Chapter 6

Becoming Grateful for Coffee

My mind was sinking into a very good place as we were driving that day. I wondered how my new friend did it. I wondered if this was the same way he helped everyone, or if he surmised exactly what I needed. I was looking at people and myself in a whole new way. I saw the perfection in everything . How could anything be judged as bad? I wondered how much that gold stuff I was taking every morning had to do with it. I wondered what it was, for that matter. I wanted to ask him if he was trying to turn me into a hippie, because I wanted no part of that. Picturing myself as a hippie made me laugh. He didn't even look up from the computer when I did, he just smiled a bit. I cheated a little and continued to search for yellow cars. I was finding more and more lately. I didn't have to say the affirmation anymore, though, because I simply felt it when I looked at people. Affirmation, I thought. I could call it that now. I wondered what he meant by "solidify the lesson." Some act of selflessness, perhaps. Some sort of challenge or a test maybe.

Whatever it was, I was up for it. I felt humble. Maybe someone was listening to my pleas for help.

We got more supplies at the superstore and he slow-cooked a pork tenderloin with small-cut potatoes in an amazing sauce and served it with asparagus. "Once this gig is over, let me know if you'd like the job as my personal chef. I'd hire you in an instant, if you'd work for food," I joked.

"What, no more fifty-fifty split?" he kidded back. "Forget it, kid, you couldn't afford me."

"How do you make your money anyway?" I asked.

"I made my money in the stock market," he said self-importantly, impersonating Thurston Howell the Third, "I'm a multimillionaire, so I mostly do it for fun now. It's quite easy once you get the hang of it."

I laughed. "Fine, don't tell me," I replied. I took this to mean that he made enough money in the stock market to support his lifestyle, meager as it was. I took another bite and said, "What if I throw in my undying gratitude?"

"We start that tomorrow too. Such an anxious student," he replied, giving me trouble.

"Can you give me a hint as to what it entails?" I asked.

He changed his tone to a very serious one as he explained, "Look, you've gotten through a huge lesson extremely fast. Most people take weeks to do what you managed to do in just a few days. You did devote a lot more time per day to it than most people have the opportunity for, but your heart was extremely ready to accept it. You're a bit further along than a lot of my students start out at. There exists a disconnect between the mind and the soul until the mind becomes free of judgment. Now that you have made the connection, your mind has to adjust. It will do a lot of this while you sleep, so we need as little input as possible. That way, your mind spends more time sorting out its new discovery than receiving even newer input. Your dreams are a powerful tool, and tonight, we're going to use them to the fullest. We are creating a unity of mind, body and soul, and skipped steps weaken this unity. So, as the chef, I say relax." Realizing how intense he must have sounded, he said his last sentence with levity.

I slept well that night and had difficulty waking up. My new friend had coffee. "It never ceases to amaze me how you can get by me without waking me," I said.

"Yeah, I am pretty amazing," he said, chuckling and handing me the coffee. "Time for school."

"I haven't even had my coffee and I've got a delivery to make," I said, expressing concern.

"You can drink your coffee during class and the lesson is short," he replied. "Just write down one thing you're grateful for and concentrate on it for at least a minute. This is a brain exercise that we will be making a habit of. There's more to it than that, but the lengthy explanation will come much later. I'll be up here waiting, but it shouldn't take long and it doesn't matter what you write. I'm not going to read it and it doesn't have to be profound. If you're grateful for coffee, then write that you're grateful for coffee. Just remember to hold on to the thought of being grateful for a while."

The paper stared at me blankly. I didn't know what to write. I wasn't sure what he wanted here, and I was a little aggravated starting so soon, as I had just woken up. So I wrote, a bit in defiance, "I'm grateful for coffee." My act of secret sarcasm made me smile. Then I started thinking about how much I like coffee and how good it made me feel to drink it. I loved it. Its aroma alone was intoxicating. I even felt a little sorry for those who could not appreciate it. The warm "good morning" it seemed to say. I was definitely grateful for coffee and silently offered my appreciation for it.

Afterward, I went out to "water the tires." This is trucker lingo for relieving oneself inconspicuously near the truck. Generally speaking, there is a gap between the cab of the truck and the trailer, by the frame, that makes for an excellent urinal if there's no one who could possibly be in line of sight from the sides. In the name of aerodynamics, skirting has eliminated this gap on many trucks.. In that case, one has to step up on the catwalk (the metal plank between the left and right sides of the frame) to take care of business. This is just one aspect of the industry that is just plain uncivilized, but one has to make the best of it. Toilets and showers, for instance, are something most people have a private or semiprivate option of. However, we get to share some of the dirtiest toilets and showers, used by people carrying germs of various kinds from all over the country. Some of the showers I've seen would scare off many people, but most of them are okay, and when you need a shower, it always makes you feel better afterwards, even if it gives you the willies during. I have seen toilets so bad that have made me resort to alternatives I prefer not to describe. My new friend was taking all of it in stride.

I got back in the truck in a flash, and we went to deliver the load. When I got backed up to the dock, I asked, "All right, are you going to explain this morning's lesson, or am I going to spend a few days on it, then have another emotional breakthrough?"

This made him laugh, and then he grinned like a cat toying with its prey before eating it. "And so, they threw the baby out with the bathwater," he said, very dramatically. I think he got a kick out of confusing me, and lived for my stares of confusion.

He continued, "There was a time when most people in this country said grace before every meal, especially dinner. They gave thanks for it. As a society, we recognized just how destructive judgment was and quietly left religion. Many did it physically, while others did it in silent spirit. Fewer are those who embraced judgment, seeing it as noble, fighting against those who see its destructive power and resent the pain it has caused in their lives, as well as the lives of others. Even then, not all of those households practice it in private, only publicly. The end result is that our society has gotten away from the act of showing gratitude on a consistent basis."

"I never thought about that," I said. "I'm confused. Why would it matter, once you free yourself from judgment? Why would the universe require praise?"

"It doesn't," he replied. He paused and then, watching the puzzled look on my face for a while, he finally twisted the knife of confusion by adding, "You do."

"Why does everything have to be so difficult with you?" I asked out of frustration.

"Things that come easily are easily dismissed," he replied.

"Okay. Why do we require praise, then?" I asked, sighing.

"I thought you'd never ask," he teased with a smile. "What one dwells upon in their thoughts becomes one's reality. If you think about yellow cars, for instance…," he raised his eyebrows for effect, "you not only start seeing more yellow cars, but you also draw more yellow cars into your life. As a society, we stopped looking for yellow cars. Many households turned off their mealtime gratitude and turned on their televisions. So instead of focusing on gratitude, which draws in more to be grateful for, they turned on cynicism, which draws in the opposite. Now they sit around wondering why everyone is so unhappy. Hence, they threw the baby out with the bathwater."

"Oh…," I said as if having a revelation, "so all I have to do is show gratitude regularly in order to be happy?" He let out a sigh of disappointment. It was a sigh I was getting used to, and I said meekly "I'm not stupid, you know."

"I know, I'm sorry," he apologized. "You're one of the brightest pupils I've had. It's just that you're so eager for answers that you're quick to jump to the wrong conclusions, that's all." He then continued his original line of thought, "All you have to do is change the way you think."

"Oh, that's all," I said sarcastically. "No problem, done by lunch."

"Right," he said, drawing it out. "It will take time, but you're a fast learner. You've heard people say that happiness is a choice?"

"Yeah," I answered.

"Well it is. But just like being skinny is a choice, one has to diet and exercise in order to make it happen. Your diet will be positive input and your exercises will be for your mind. I will be your dietitian and trainer, so to speak."

"Ah, that makes sense," I said. I was getting used to these miniature revelations.

"The first order of business – besides starting the habit of gratitude, of course – is to make sure the first lesson sticks. In order for your mind to solidify what you've learned, you have to teach it to somebody else," he explained.

"Who?" I said, puzzled once again. I had visions of going up to total strangers, espousing my newly learned lesson and being less than well received, to say the least.

"Online," he replied.

"On that question-and-answer site you go to?" I asked.

"That very one," he said. "It's the greatest thing since the internet itself as far as a teaching tool. If Internet is inaccessible, it can be done by imagining someone who needs help and then answering their questions in front of one's imaginary audience. But you will have the pleasure of helping real people and your answers will be read by a real audience. It is infinitely more powerful. I even set you up with a screen name to drive the point across. What do you think?" He was positively giddy.

"I think you're a bit off," I said giving him trouble. "I don't know if I'm ready yet. I may end up doing more harm than good."

"You'll be fine. Remember, most of these people have no idea how destructive judgment is. They have no clue the damage it's doing to their psyche. Any help you can offer will be better than what most people can. And besides," he said with a sigh, "people won't accept it until they're ready, and most of the people you present your gift of knowledge to, including your audience, won't be ready. The thing is, though, you'll never know the impact you have made. There may be one person who happens to read what you have written and it completely changes their life for the better. These are the ripples that we teachers often refer too. Your ripples will be largely unseen by you, but are far more important than you realize. Ripples are far more important than most people realize. And remember, intention is supported by the universe, so you will be helped."

"I need help, that's for sure," I said jokingly. A knock at the door startled me. It was the receiver with my bills. They were finished with me. I don't know why, at so many of the places I go to, they feel it necessary to bang on the door real hard. They wouldn't go to someone's house and bang on the door like you see on police raid shows, but it happens frequently with my truck. I don't know if they are taking their frustrations out on my door or if they're in a huge hurry. Maybe there are a lot of drivers who will sleep through anything else, so they just start out at a high intensity. All I know is that my mood dampens quickly when it happens.

"Thank you. Have a nice day," I managed. After he was out of earshot, I continued, "Jackass." My new friend laughed at this.

Chapter 7

Room Service

I called into dispatch and found out that I would be picking up in the area Monday, so I was done for the week. It was unusual for me to be ending my week so early, but I wasn't going to complain. According to the Department of Transportation, a driver can drive no more than seventy hours in an eight-day period and this becomes reset after an off-duty period of thirty-four hours, which is twenty-four hours plus a ten-hour break (at least I think that's how they arrived at that number).

"Well, we're done for the week," I said.

"So, what now?" he replied.

"Well usually I either hang out at the truck stop or get a hotel room. The hotel room is tax deductible and since I actually have someone to hang out with, coupled with the fact that I'd like to get out of this truck for a while—being a bit more cramped than usual—I suggest we go that route. Can you go half with me on one?" I asked.

"I can do better than that. As I mentioned, I travel a lot and this is one of the towns I was led to in order to help someone else get to where they needed to go. I don't usually stay with the people I help, so I find myself in hotel rooms quite often. But I know the perfect place. It doesn't have truck parking, though," he explained.

I was a bit leery of the type of place he might stay in, given the simplicity of his lifestyle, but he was very clean. "All right," I said, "how about I pay for the cab if you pay for the hotel." I neglected to tell him that St. Louis was a town I was familiar with, too, and knew exactly where I could park a truck in most areas.

"Done," he said. He got online, found the number and made the reservation. I found us a place to park very close to the hotel, but it was still just outside of walking distance. It was a safe place, well lit and in an industrial area near the nicer side of town. I had parked here before and was reasonably comfortable with my choice. I still did my best to cover the stuff I was leaving there to lessen temptation. A driver has to be a cognoscente of many things when he leaves a tractor trailer somewhere. Not only are there the usual safety issues of possible break-in and vandalism, but there's the risk of being ticketed and towed. Everything is more expensive when it comes to big rigs, usually five to ten times. If a ticket costs twenty dollars for a car, it might cost two hundred for a big truck. The same goes for toll roads as well. A friend of mine had his truck towed from the parking lot of a closed-down department store and it cost him over three thousand dollars to get it out. He was only there long enough to eat and do laundry. I guess they view tractor trailers as a business and charge accordingly. The problem is, a company driver (or employee) is the one who foots the bill, save for tolls, of course. It does seem, at times, like all of the world hates a truck driver, or at least sees us as an absolute nuisance. I will be the first to admit that when driving a car, I see the trucks themselves as a bit of a nuisance—they move slowly, obstruct your view, etc. But you wouldn't believe the number of places I pick up and deliver to that treat us—well quite frankly—inhumanely. I've stood outside at a window in negative-twenty-degree weather waiting for the people inside to finish their conversations so that I could get my paperwork and be on my way. I'll never forget that day because they didn't allow drivers to use the restrooms indoors, either, and when I went into the portable toilet, the door slammed shut behind me and just shattered. In a lot of places, as soon as you walk into the warehouse, you find yourself in a cage, begging to get someone's attention. Nevertheless, I always greet the shippers and receivers with a smile and act very friendly and courteous, regardless of how they treat me. I tend to see the best in people, and I assume that if someone at one of these places is short with me, a frustrated driver who couldn't hold his temper was responsible for rubbing them the wrong way. Sometimes it gets to me, though, but having someone to hang out with was helping my mood considerably.

The cab driver must have been nearby because we didn't have to wait long. Arriving at the hotel, I was relieved to see that it was very nice. Everyone there seemed to recognize Matt and lit up when they saw him, giving him warm greetings. They quickly grabbed my shabby travel bag and the grocery bags of perishable food, leaving me feeling a bit embarrassed, but the people were so friendly I quickly forgot about it. This was a far cry from what I was used to. I looked around a bit while Matt checked us in. It was a very nice hotel. I felt like maybe he was getting the short end of the stick on our deal, but this was his choice, so I didn't feel bad for long. The bellhop escorted us up to our room, which I thought was rather silly, since we had very little in the way of baggage. When we got to the room, my jaw dropped. I was expecting to see a small room with a couple of beds in it; not only was it quite a large room, but I didn't see any beds. There was a kitchen and bar area where the restroom usually is and couches and chairs where the beds usually go. There was even a great big desk area. There were two separate bedrooms to this place, too, each having an elaborate bathroom with separate tubs and showers. This was more like a luxury apartment than a hotel room. And the view was amazing. I contained my excitement as much as I could and put the food in the fridge, while Matt signed something and handed it to the bellhop. This was, of course, after he went through the whole spiel about the amenities and what not. "I don't suppose you brought your swimsuit," I joked, trying to hide my being completely overwhelmed.

"No, but we can pick one up at the store," he said, matter-of-factly. "As you pointed out, I'm due for a change in my look anyway, so I'll pick up some more appropriate travel wear as well. What about you? Do you have a swimsuit?"

"What about me? What about you? What is all this?" I questioned, not being able to contain myself any longer.

"I told you I was a multimillionaire, why do you seem so surprised?" he answered.

"Yeah, I didn't really believe that, but that's almost beside the point. It just doesn't add up. Nothing about you thus far has led me to believe that you lead anything but a modest lifestyle. I mean, you even had me pay the cab fare over here," I stated in peeved bewilderment. "Don't get me wrong, I'm grateful for you forking over the cash for a place like this, but it doesn't make sense."

He laughed. "I had a feeling you'd take it about like this. As a teacher, I find it best to keep my student on their toes," he explained with a smirk. "The truth is that when I discovered that what you think about becomes your reality, I flooded my thoughts with that of wealth and material objects. This, of course, led me to do things that created great wealth. Once I obtained all of the things I wanted in life, I realized that I didn't really need them and many of them were more trouble than they were worth. Owning things started owning me. I realized that mostly what I liked about that stuff in the first place was the experience, and I already experienced it. Not that there's anything wrong with owning stuff, it just wouldn't allow me to do what I truly wanted to do. I truly love helping people in this very unique and direct way, completely trusting the universe to guide me. It really frees my soul. So I sold all of the stuff and gave half to charity, while keeping the rest in my bank account to travel with. I replace it occasionally with what I make in the stock market. I afford myself the luxury of staying in nice places without having to concern myself with hiring staff or paying property taxes or any of the other headaches. It helps me relax and rejuvenate to continue doing what I do."

I could kind of understand what he was talking about, but I was still a bit puzzled. "Okay, so why then did I have to pick up cab fare?" I questioned.

"That was for your benefit," he replied.

"This keeping-me-on-my-toes thing gets a bit tiring at times," I stated, knowing he would understand that I needed further explanation.

"It's a bit hard to explain, but essentially everyone needs to pay their own way in life in order to have peace of mind. Even those who can't, feel better if you help them feel as if they contribute somehow. It's an ingrained part of the human psyche. People often do a grave disservice to others by not recognizing this," he explained. "A nice dip in the tub should help you relax. That's what I'm doing. We can get clothes and swimsuits for the semiprivate pool and hot tub later. Right now we need a break from each other anyway."

"Is that your way of telling me you're getting sick of me?" I asked.

"Wouldn't you get tired of all these questions?" he joked, raising his eyebrows. "Aren't you tired of being on your toes all day for that matter?"

"Fair enough, I'll be in my room," I replied. I was tired and definitely ready to stop thinking for a while. The tub was amazing and I slipped into a thought coma as I eased into its nice warm water. I laughed at everything as I told the bathtub that it was perfect and beautiful and I loved it. After a while, I showered and took a nap.

I awoke to the sound of the TV in the other room. It was tuned to a news channel, which was discussing the stock market. Bleary-eyed, I walked in to a smile and an offer of a beer. The beer I obliged, the smile I could not yet return. "Funny, isn't it?" he asked.

"What's that?" I returned.

"You could almost make a living doing the opposite of what these so-called market analysts suggest you do," he answered.

"How do you do what you do in the market anyway?" I asked.

He laughed, "It's so easy you wouldn't believe me."

"I think I have enough trust in you now. Try me," I replied.

"All right, it's very simple. I just do what the smartest investors do," he said with a smile rewarding his own brilliance.

"Aren't these guys on TV intelligent? I mean they are paid to give their opinions on a show that airs all over the country," I said.

"Sometimes they have the brilliant traders on, and they usually spend all their time questioning them as if they're crazy. It's a hoot. We have a tendency to do that. When everyone is saying the same thing over and over again about how you should do something, it's usually wrong," he explained. "Well, you remember this in the lesson about judgment. One has to love others in order to love oneself—exactly the opposite of what most people rattle off. These guys on TV get paid to rattle off what most people are thinking. They get paid for popular opinion. If their opinions weren't popular, they wouldn't have an audience. If you want to get ahead in any aspect of life, emulate the most successful in their field, not the most popular ones."

"So you're not a popular guy then?" I joked, giving him trouble.

He laughed so hard he spit out some of his beer. As he was wiping his chin, he said, "Are you kidding? The question-and-answer site that I go to selects a best answer. Either the asker chooses one or it goes to a vote. My percentage of best answers is about twenty percent, and it would be less that that if I didn't cheat in the beginning."

"Cheat?" I questioned.

"Yeah, I would make up screen names to get more votes for my answers. I thought it would add weight to what I suggested and help more people," he chuckled at his own logic. "As I said before, we all have our lessons to learn. I guess I'm still not fully cured, though. Whenever there's a tie, I'll vote myself in." He was smiling, amused with himself. Seeing the confusion in my eyes he added, "Enjoy being human, it is delightful in its nature."

"Speaking of being human, I don't know how up to shopping I am," I said, sipping my beer.

"Oh, thank goodness," he agreed. "I don't know how you do this all the time. It's exhausting. Let's order in room service."

"I have a better idea. Let's get some of that St. Louis style pizza and toasted ravs," I suggested.

"Toasted ravs?" he questioned.

"Yeah, toasted ravioli, it's a St. Louis thing. The pizza has a cheese unique to it as well, and it's on a very thin crust cut into squares. I like it but I don't really think of pizza when I eat it. It's kind of an interesting take. I can't believe you didn't try it when you were here."

"I ate mostly room service. It's very good here. Like yourself, I eat alone a lot, so I don't get too elaborate with things. Makes me feel a bit lonely," he said.

"Yeah, I've opted for the easier choice quite a few times because I didn't have anyone to share it with," I said, sounding a bit sad. But I changed my mood quickly and said, "Tonight, we feast," and held up my beer to toast.

"We need more beer, too. There were only two in the bar. I'll call room service for that," he said, reaching for the phone.

"So that's how rich people drink," I joked, using my best hick accent, "Us poor folk do something we call a beer run."

"Hold on a sec," he said into the phone and then covered the mouthpiece, "I'll be happy to negate my order if you would like to do the honors. I think I saw a convenience store a few blocks from here."

"Room service it is then," I replied, not wanting to call his bluff. "I'll order the pizza online." He continued to order up a six-pack of beer and I ordered the food.

"While you're online, you should check out the answer site," he suggested. "I put it on the favorites bar."

I thought that a bit presumptuous of him, but I was a little excited to check it out. "All right, give me a sec to finish the order. Anything else you want, like a salad or something?"

"No, I'll just try whatever you're having, so order extra for me," he replied.

I finished the order and went to the answer site. It seemed a bit overwhelming with all of the questions. Everything from how tight to torque the bolts of the head of an engine once you replace the gasket, to what should I get a three-year-old boy for his birthday. Then

I noticed topics in a box at the top. "Where do you go to find the type of questions you want me to answer?" I asked.

"I get them from a couple of places," he explained, "in 'Arts and Humanities,' you'll find the philosophy section, and some really good ones will be in 'Family and Relationships.'"

"Oh, I see it," I mumbled as I was perusing the questions. Wow, there were a lot of questions. "You know there's a religion and spirituality section?"

"Oh yeah," he said excitedly, "Check that section out. I kind of forgot about it. I never go there because it's just a battleground for the God-is-the-answer-to-everything crowd versus there-is-no-God crowd."

"Why would people who don't believe in God even go there?" I wondered aloud.

"Judgment," he replied. "Many of those people have an anger in their hearts because they see the result of just how destructive judgment is. Maybe they've even been affected by it directly. A lot of homosexuals, for instance, often have a strong resentment toward religious beliefs that damn them simply for being who they are. The people that carry these resentments often don't realize that they're doing the same judging that they see as so destructive. They don't recognize judgment itself as the problem, they just see it as misguided. So you have one group judging and another group judging the judgers. It's such a vicious cycle that I had almost no success there.

Many of the questions there are asked simply to push an agenda, not because the asker is seeking answers."

"Great," I said sarcastically. "You want me answer questions where it's almost certain I won't be helping anyone and I may be villainized as well—good times."

"Generally, there's no specific feedback, just thumbs-down marks," he said.

I couldn't find anything relatable to what I had learned, and after reading some of the questions and answers aloud to him, he commented that it was still a circus and relented to my starting in philosophy. Sometimes I wondered about him. I seemed to place a lot of faith in a guy who makes a lot of mistakes. He was supposed to be helping me grow spiritually, yet here we were sharing beers together while he's not sure what section I should be doing my homework in. Doesn't seem like a recipe for spiritual growth. If I hadn't already seen major results, I would have abandoned his methods and settled for his company. I laughed to myself as I realized I was once again judging. I guess I did have a ways to go.

I found myself answering questions that had nothing to do with the lessons I had learned at first. I never realized how many people have trouble with the basics of life and relationships. It was fun doling out advice to people who obviously needed it. Then I came across a suicide question. It was someone quite distraught about life, describing in detail all her woes. I felt sorry for her. As I was deciding as to whether or not this non-judgment stuff could help her, our pizza and beer arrived.

As we cracked open another beer and started in on the food, I said, "I came across a question from someone contemplating suicide," hoping this would be enough to elicit a response.

"Wow, this is good," he said, referring to the pizza.

"What should I do?" I asked.

"What do you mean what should you do? You're supposed to be answering questions, so answer it," he replied.

"Yeah, but this is serious," I said.

"Do you not think you could help this person?" he asked.

"Maybe, but I can't be responsible for life and death," I said.

"You're not responsible for that, only for trying to help," he explained. "Do you think you can help this person with what you've learned?"

"Maybe," I replied.

"Then try," he said. "Most of the people answering will not have near the perspective you do and many of them shirk the responsibility and shift it to a hotline number. You may be that whisper in someone's ear that turns their whole life around. What did you call these things again?"

"Toasted ravioli," I replied, "or ravs."

"Oh yeah, ravs. They're very good," he said. "Don't take these things too seriously. Answer seriously, of course, but you're not responsible for anyone's actions but your own, and trying to help is a noble action. Besides, you need a lot of practice. What you think about becomes your reality. The more you drill this into your head by writing it over and over again, the more it becomes your reality. The teacher is the student."

"You sure I won't be messing anyone up in the process, though?" I asked.

"Well, you never know," he replied with a grin.

"All right," I sighed.

"You can help people if you believe you can," he said. "A little less doubt and a little more faith—remember, your thoughts make up your reality."

So with that, I washed my hands and went back to the computer. I had eaten enough and I was excited to get started. I went through and explained how destructive judgment is and how to free herself from it as I had. I used the lion example and went through all the details of my own experience. When I was satisfied with my answer, I clicked send.

"My first answer using what I learned about judgment," I said, beaming with pride. "Want to read it?"

"Yeah, let me take a look," he replied, leaning over me to read. "Well, let's see here. Good. Good. Nice. Very well worded. So you were paying attention. Excellent job." As he started to walk away he added, "Just one thing, though…"

"Oh?" I wondered aloud.

"Those are my words," he said.

"I thought that was kind of the point," I replied.

He took a sip of his beer, looked away from the TV and said, "No, the point is to put the lesson in your own terms. When the lesson becomes uniquely yours, it will have the greatest impact on you and others. I can tell that you understand what I've taught you by what I've read, so it shouldn't be that difficult. You don't need to come up with all new words or anything, but you need to use examples that speak from your heart. Try a few different ones till you think you have one that works well for you. Determine your style, don't just reiterate mine. There are plenty of people for you to try your ideas out on. That's why I think this site is such a useful tool in training. Don't worry, though, you'll get the hang of it, practice, practice, practice," he said with a grin. "You know you don't have to do it tonight."

"I'm kind of enjoying this, actually," I said.

"I kind of thought you might," he replied. "It feels good helping people when you have the answers, doesn't it?" He smiled a warm smile.

"I knew you had to get something out of this," I teased.

"All acts are somewhat selfish," he stated, "including this one. You're on your own. Good night." With that, he went to bed.

The next morning I awoke to the sound of "ah." As I realized the sound was emanating from Matt, I slumped back down on the soft pillows. This hotel room was a far cry from some of the dumps I had been in before. At some of the places, upon waking, the first thing I'd want to do is get out of bed and try not think about where I had just slept. One of the places I slept in took a lot of mind-over-matter to fall asleep. The company I was working for at the time paid for the room while my truck was being worked on. I wondered why the guy explained to me that one of the hotels was booked up and did I mind staying at the other one. I understood the expression on his face the moment I walked into the room. Although it was a reputable chain, it was not a reputable neighborhood, and I learned that makes a big difference. I found a French fry on the bathroom floor, which is not so bad in and of itself, but it's a good indicator of how well the room was cleaned if they managed to miss something as obvious as that. There was something crusty on the sheets, like paint or something. You could tell they had been washed, so I kept telling myself that whatever it was, it was sterile. I remember checking out the next morning and a fellow survivor and I had a support group meeting. He explained that his pillow smelled of urine as he burst into tears and put his head on my shoulder. Okay, maybe we just exchanged words of disgust, but the pillow smell complaint was real.

This, on the other hand, was a room that was a delight to wake up in. I enjoyed my cozy environment for a while until my thoughts turned to coffee. I fumbled my way into the kitchen area, listening to Matt sitting and humming away an "ah" sound and started some coffee. It was one of those individual-serving coffee makers. I never liked those because they don't allow for one to regulate the strength of coffee, and I like my coffee strong. "Good morning, sleeping beauty," he said.

"Good morning," I replied.

"Sleep well?" he asked.

"Oh yeah," I replied. "You want some coffee?"

"Nah, I had some earlier downstairs with breakfast. The coffee's better in the restaurant," he explained.

"Lucky dog," I said. "How come you didn't wake me?"

"I figured you needed to sleep, you've been through a lot. Training your mind can be exhausting," he said.

"Yeah, well I was up pretty late answering questions, or should I say early," I said. "It seems now, though, that I have more questions than answers."

"That's kind of a hazard of self-exploration," he said with a smile. "It's all good, though. Most of the answers will find you as you start to become more in line with your true self. Why don't you throw one at me just for fun and I'll give you my perspective."

He never fit my expectations. I thought he was supposed to give me the answers or point me in the right direction so I could figure them out. All the religious leaders had answers for everything and could point to something as a reference. I had to think of a good one, so I gave him one I was baffled with. "Do you need to learn the reason behind your behavior in order to change it?" I asked. "It seems like a lot of people think it's important to understand why they act like they do in order to change. I mean, isn't that what psychology is all about?"

"I don't know; I teach people how to swim," he said.

"Why do you have to do that all the time? Can't you just answer a simple question without making me work for the answer? You have no idea how frustrating that is," I said.

"I don't do it for my benefit," he said, looking at one of those local attraction-type magazines that hotels are famous for having. "Sooner or later you're going to have to figure these things out for yourself. I'm just helping you by giving you clues so you can start the process on your own. I've walked you through some answers. How about you walk me through this one? What could I possibly mean by that?"

"Swimming?!" I said with frustration. I put my face in my hands and thought. "You teach swimming…" I contemplated this for a few moments and then continued, "In order to swim, don't you need to know why you previously weren't able to." I looked to him for approval.

"What are you looking at me for?" he asked. "You're doing fine."

"So there is no benefit to understanding why we are the way we are," I continued. "We can change our behaviors irrespective of our past which in turn changes our future, allowing us to become swimmers."

"Very good," he said. "But I wouldn't say that there is no benefit. It's just that so many people honestly believe that if they can just figure out what went wrong in their past that made them the way they are, they can somehow fix it so that they can be the person they want to be. This is tantamount to spending all of your time studying the physics behind swimming instead of going to the local pool and learning to swim."

"Okay, that makes sense, but I have another question for you," I said. "What were you doing when I came in?"

"Oh, that's a meditation thing. It helps to bring in that which you desire. In this case, the energy to put up with a student like you," he replied, grinning.

"You need to teach me it so I'll have the energy to put up with you," I said.

"Is that the best you could come up with?" he said. "You've really got to work on your retorts."

"Are you ready to go, 'cause I'm getting hungry and we have shopping to do," I asked in frustration.

"Yeah, I found out there's a train we can catch about half a mile from here that goes to the local mall," he said. "Still not sure what look I'll go for."

"I'm thinking either beach attire or the safari look would work," I suggested. "Beachwear expresses a peace about life, while safari expresses your traveling adventure side."

"From the way you describe me, it sounds like Australian wear might be the way to go, kind of a cross between the two, eh, mate?" he said the last couple of words with a horrid accent and continued in that accent. "Maybe even feign the accent to pick up the ladies. What do you think?"

I looked at him like he was crazy and said, "I think that accent would drive them away. I couldn't even use you as a decent wingman. That accent would kill my chances by association. The look might work for you, though."

"Maybe I just need to practice the ol' accent," he said, using that same horrid accent.

"As long as I don't have to be subjected to it," I stated. "By the way, I used the last of that stuff this morning."

"The white powder gold?" he asked.

"Yeah, I guess we need to pick some more up today," I said.

He laughed. "You don't just go to the corner drugstore and pick that stuff up, you know," he explained.

"Well, I figured that, but I'm sure they have a metaphysical-type store in this town," I said.

He smiled and said, "I don't think you understand. That stuff is made using an alchemical process that turns gold into an ingestible form. There not that many people who know how to do that and it's not exactly done on a large-scale basis. There are cheap versions sold in some vitamin stores but they simply use a source where ORMEs occur naturally. They do not attempt to extract the ORMEs in any way. There are many places that do extract ORMEs from sources other than gold that are very good, but I have yet to find them in a health-food or metaphysical store."

"So that's it, then?" I asked.

"That's it," he replied. "Don't look so disappointed. You don't need it to further your growth. In fact, it wasn't necessary at all. It just helps a little."

"I figure I need all the help I can get," I said with a sigh of disappointment.

He opened the door and as we walked to the elevator, he said, "Here's a question for you. Why do all of my students get discouraged with their progress so easily? Pretend you're answering it on that site."

"Learning something new is like getting on an elevator," I said, a bit defiantly, then tried to make it work. "When you first start out you can see the floor numbers changing, but you really have no idea if the elevator is actually taking you to the floor you want to go to until you arrive. Unlike the elevator, however, learning something new takes much longer, so it can get discouraging at times. Your students see themselves as trapped in the elevator and have to take your word that the numbers mean something."

"Very good," he said as we arrived at our floor. "So how do I keep them from getting discouraged?"

"You're going to have to entertain them in the elevator," I replied.

"Very good," he said as we walked outside. He walked at a more leisurely pace than I did, and I found myself having to slow down. "Although we have a destination, the journey is a part of the overall experience. If you can learn to appreciate the journey as much as the destination, you will find all of life interesting. You have mastered this in your profession, have you not?"

"I suppose so. It's still nice to be entertained along the way, though. I tune in to talk stations on the radio sometimes to pass the time," I replied.

"Well, I have some entertainment planned for tomorrow, but formal attire is required," he said.

"I don't really do formal attire. Not only do I not have any, but also functions that require it are not really my scene. Maybe we should go to the zoo or something," I suggested.

He could see the look of concern on my face and addressed it, "Don't worry about not having proper attire, we're going to the mall where we can get a couple of suits. I promise that it will be very entertaining, and it will do you some good to be in the company of successful people. I wouldn't take you somewhere you wouldn't enjoy." He could tell that he wasn't getting anywhere with reassuring me, so he added, "You're just going to have to trust me on this. I haven't steered you wrong thus far, have I?"

"No, but," I started, but then seeing the look on his face let me know that I wasn't getting out of it. "You really want to buy suits just for this?"

"Of course, and afterward we can donate them," he said, smiling.

"I'm not donating mine," I said with concern.

He laughed, "Don't worry, I'm buying yours too."

"Hey, don't laugh at me, you're the one that said all this mumbo jumbo about paying my own way," I said.

"This is something I'm hosting—that's different," he explained, still chuckling a bit.

"You sure do have a lot of rules," I said, shaking my head.

"Don't worry, you get to buy lunch at the food court," he said.

"If we ever get there," I chided.

"Relax," he said. He had a way of saying it that actually caused me to relax. I wasn't looking forward to going to some swanky place that required a suit, and I found myself actually stressed about it. I'm sure he had no issue with it because he was probably used to hanging around wealthy people, but something about rich people brings out my insecurities. Quite frankly, they intimidate me. Yet he had a way about him that was very calming, soothing, almost, and I was drifting into acceptance of it. Besides it was tomorrow, a world away, and I was enjoying our walk.

When we got to the mall, we immediately went to the suit store, so that if alterations were required, they could be done while we shopped. I really had a difficult time seeing Matt in a suit. Although it didn't seem like him, he wore it as if he owned it. I felt as awkward as he seemed to feel comfortable. While they were doing alterations, we went to eat in the food court. Afterward we headed to get shoes and finally to a more casual store to find swimsuits and a new look for Matt. The swimsuits were easy to pick out, but his look took a while. I had a hard time picturing him in any kind of clothes other than what he wore. I even started laughing loudly at some of the outfits he brought out. I think he was even playing this up for comic relief. Eventually, he decided on white pants and a matching white shirt. I expressed my concerns that white was not a great color for traveling, but it did look natural on him, and he said that it wouldn't be an issue. It actually seemed a natural transition since the material was loose- fitting. It wasn't too far from the pajama look he had before and, somehow, white seemed fitting for someone as aware as he. It also could have been standard issue clothing at an insane asylum if it was a little more hospital-esque, which just might fit his personality as well.

We gathered our—or should I say his—purchases and headed for the hotel. It felt a bit weird carrying suits and bags on the train, but was even less fun walking with them. By the time we got back to the hotel room I was ready for a nap, but wanted to see if anyone responded to my answers last night on the answer website, so I went straight to the computer. There were a couple of people who had chosen my answers as best but for the most part, not a lot of response. Clearly I wasn't going to get out of this as much as I had put in. I worked really hard on those answers and the only good thing to come from it was that I was a little discouraged, which made for good sleeping. It always seemed easier to sleep when I was a bit sad. So I informed Matt that I would be napping and he asked if I wouldn't mind if he looked over my answers. I said I'd actually like that—thinking maybe at least he could appreciate them—and I was off to sleep.

I awoke about an hour later and we decided to go swimming and use the hot tub. It felt good to relax. There's something about water that's so relaxing and it was nice that there weren't many people around. We stayed till we looked like prunes and finally meandered our way back to the hotel room. We ordered more beer and room service since neither of us wanted to go out. He was right about the room service being good there. It was quite nice. "You seem to have good writing skills," he said. "I was impressed."

"You seemed to be one of the few," I responded.

He looked up from his meal and made sure to have eye contact when he said, "You'd be amazed at the amount of people you help that you never know about. Then there's the ripple effect. You know, you affect someone and they in turn affect someone." He looked at me knowingly.

"Yeah, you helped me, I helped someone else. I get it," I replied. "But that doesn't necessarily mean that the ripples have a positive effect."

"Oh?" he said curiously.

"Yeah, someone could have taken what I said the wrong way and the ripples could be harming people as well, right?" I asked.

"Intention," he said dramatically. "What have I told you from the beginning? The universe supports intention. The intentional waves grow greater in strength, unintentional grow weaker. The universe supports intention."

"Okay, then what about negative intentions? Don't they create negative ripples?" I asked.

"Negative intentions are just as supported by the universe, but we are directly affected by the ripples we make. So whatever intent we send out, we experience. The creation of our realities begins with thought. This is why it's so important to give your thoughts intention," he explained. "This is what you did when you used the affirmations. You were telling your subconscious mind the reality you wanted to create. It then went to work to create that reality for you." I sat there looking puzzled for a moment, then I had a look of revelation and started to say something, but quickly switched back to the puzzled look.

"Don't worry, it seeps in a little at a time," he said, smiling.

"I thought you said they were proclamations?" I said, puzzled.

"That was the intent you needed at the time," he replied.

"It sounds like this is just all about affirmations, then," I said in the gentlest way I could. I didn't want to sound disrespectful.

"No," he said with great patience, "It's about intent. Look, this will become clearer over time. Right now you need to focus on getting your first lesson very clear. I suggest you get back to answering questions.

We have a big day tomorrow and we'll need to get up kind of early. I'm retiring to my room for the evening. Good night."

I bid him goodnight and went back to the questions. I found it to be a lot of fun. Every time I answered a question it came a bit easier to me. I didn't seem to get much in the way of feedback, so I tried using personal experience by explaining my personal revelation. My teacher (I guess I could call him that now) would probably think I was wasting my time on some of the questions because I answered them just for fun. They were personal opinion–type questions. I found myself losing track of time answering questions, and realized I needed to get to bed.

Chapter 8

Shish KeRob

When morning came I was awakened abruptly. "Time to get up," he said, throwing open the curtains. I quickly hid my eyes and groaned in complaint. "Come on. The boys at the club will be expecting us soon." Again, that earned him a grunt of complaint. "Trust me, you don't want to walk in late to this."

"All right, all right, I'm awake. Just give me a minute," I pleaded.

"Okay. We leave in forty-five minutes. Coffee's on if you want some," and with that he left the room.

Even though I was used to being woken up in an aggravating fashion, I'm still not a fan, and I was glad coffee was on. After getting ready, we headed to wherever we were going. Luckily, the hotel shuttled us to the train, but I was still nervous and a little uncomfortable being out of my element. My only solace was that at least I looked good in a suit. I noticed we were going over the river into Illinois. "We're going to Illinois?" I asked with concern. I wasn't extremely familiar with the Illinois side of the St. Louis area, but I

had been cautioned to avoid it if possible. "Yes," he replied, putting his hand on my shoulder, "I know you're out of your element, but you need to be. If you do the things you've always done, you'll be at the same place you've always been. You wanted me to take you someplace else and that I am doing. Remember that this is all for your benefit and I wouldn't steer you wrong." He closed his eyes and slowly took a deep breath. "Now take a deep breath."

"I'm not sure I can," I said, pulling my collar away from my neck.

"Why do you always send me the crybabies?" he again asked the universe.

"If you're getting the same reaction from all your students, perhaps the issue is in the mirror," I countered.

"Ahhh, there's the brilliance I saw in you. Welcome back," he exclaimed. This made me smile and let go a little bit. "I have a feeling you're going to enjoy today. This is our stop."

Looking around, my nervousness started coming back. We were not in a good neighborhood. It was a mix of run-down residential and run-down industrial. I was glad that there weren't a lot of people around, and then I became nervous that there weren't a lot of people around. I wondered to myself just where we could be going around here. Was there some kind of secret society meeting that used an area of poverty as camouflage? Surely, we weren't going to serve in a soup kitchen in suits. We walked quickly, which didn't hurt my feelings any, but we paused at a gentleman begging for money long enough for Matt to hand him a dollar. The man blessed him for his kindness as we continued. "I thought you were all about everyone contributing and whatnot. What was that?" I asked.

"Compassion needs to be shown for those who refuse to be humble," he replied. "It is a difficult battle to fight when you are your own worst enemy." He saw my completely puzzled look and then said, "Oh look, we're here," as if to dodge the question.

Oh no, I thought as I looked at the place, my expression souring. He had dragged me to a church, of all places. Why did he take me here? He was right to leave me in the dark on this one, though, because I would never have agreed to this. The boys at the club, I thought as I shook my head. I stopped dead in my tracks and with the stern look I shot him, Matt knew I would need even more convincing. "Relax, I'm not converting you," he assured with a big smile. "One of my former students is the preacher here. I thought it would be good for you to witness what Christianity looks like without judgment."

"I'm not sure I'm ready enough to view it without judgment," I said. "I think you have more faith in me than I have in mys—"

"No," he interrupted. "I mean, view it being presented without judgment." He stared at my now extremely puzzled look and added, "That's the look that I live for," while grinning from ear to ear.

"I starting to think you just love torturing people," I said, relaxing a bit about the situation I found myself in. "It's very frustrating, you know."

"I know, but it's so damned effective. If it wasn't, I wouldn't do it. Everything I do has a purpose, including this," he explained, gesturing toward the church.

"All right," I relented and followed him toward the building. I didn't exactly want to walk back in this neighborhood alone anyway. You wouldn't know it was a church if it weren't for the painting of stained glass toward the top. I guess actual stained glass might be an issue in this neighborhood, so it was painted on the side of the building as if it were a window pattern. The last of the people shuffled in while we were talking, so we made our way in and found some seats in the back. Being the only white people in the crowd drew less attention than I would have imagined, and several people welcomed us to the church with warm smiles.

The singing was similar to that depicted in movies and television about churches with a predominantly black congregation, but less professionally orchestrated. Nevertheless, the enthusiasm was still there and it was inspiring. When everything settled down and we all took our seats, the preacher stood up in front of everyone with a smile on his face and started welcoming everyone to the service. Scanning the room, he noticed us sitting in the back and his smile widened as his eyes lit up. He threw out some loud words of praise and then started his sermon.

I found myself enjoying his sermon, even though I was a bit fidgety in my suit. It certainly was a new experience, but then again, this was all a new experience. The churches I had been to as a kid always read the Bible more like a rule book than anything else. Their Bibles were always marked up with passages that explained why you shouldn't do this or should do that. They always seemed to be trying to be perfect in the eyes of God, and it seemed that the more they tried, the further they got. Actually, I did too. I finally got so far away that I started searching for answers elsewhere. I couldn't see how God could be so petty that if I didn't believe that a guy who lived here on earth long ago was his one and only son and accept him as my savior, I would perish for eternity. That didn't sound like divinity to me at all. But this guy didn't seem to present it like that. In fact, he sounded a bit like my Matt.

When he finished his sermon and was about to dismiss the congregation, he mentioned that a very dear friend of his, without whom he would not be here, was in the back and suggested that everyone say hello to us along with himself as they left. I was really not prepared for this, but everyone was so friendly that it actually felt good. After everyone had made it out, Matt and the preacher hugged each other. I don't know that I've seen a smile as big as the one that man had.

My friend then introduced me as his newest student and the preacher as Robert, his former student.

"Really nice to meet you, Khris," he said with a smile. "Did you enjoy the sermon?"

"Yeah, I really did. It was quite unique," I replied. "Though it took me by surprise."

"Oh?" he questioned.

"Yeah, my friend here didn't let me know where we were going, so it was a total surprise," I said, glaring at Matt.

He laughed at that and turned to Matt saying, "Still up to your old tricks, huh?" Matt gave him a big, knowing smile. "Yeah, of course you are," he continued. "You guys busy today?"

The preacher saw the look of not knowing on my face and directed his attention to Matt.

Matt replied, "No. I was kinda hoping maybe you weren't either so we could hang out a while."

"Good, then I'll take you guys to lunch. Just give me a couple of minutes to get everything buttoned up here and we'll be on our way. Did you drive?" Robert asked.

"No, we took the train in from Missouri," Matt replied.

"Here, let me open the car for you, then," he said, pointing his car keys toward a Mercedes that made the usual blinking-light notification, letting us know which car to go to. Walking over to the car, I mentioned to my friend that the soul-saving business must be good.

"Really," he stretched as if disappointed in me. "Did you not see the church we came out of?"

"Yeah," I replied. "Can't be much for rent there."

"At least he didn't say it in front of Robert," Matt said as if talking to someone else.

"What?" I questioned with a puzzled look. I knew it would have been rude to say in front of Robert, but how could Matt not be curious?

"Mental note…address money issues…priority one," he said aloud. "That congregation doesn't supply enough money to keep the lights on. Robert owns that building and has to make up the difference in expenses with his own money. He did get a great deal on it, though, and got volunteers to help make it habitable again, but it's not supporting him. He's supporting it."

"Oh, so you millionaires keep together?" I asked.

"Robert's hardly a millionaire yet, but he might be on his way by now. When I met him he was living in his van selling food out of the back of it. He could barely afford a shower at the truck stop."

"Truck stop?" I questioned.

"Yeah, he used the CB to advertise so he could avoid paying rent for parking. He would just drive right up to the truck. He had quite the reputation with truckers," he continued.

"Wait a minute," I said with recognition, "I think I remember that guy. I didn't order from him because I was nervous about eating food served from the back of a van, but I do remember drivers talking about how good it was. Man, that's wild. I remember having a CB and listening to him say, 'For good food, go to two two.' He was famous for that line." I had said it in the same rhyming fashion as I had heard it back then. The "two two" part was referring to the CB channel twenty-two, of course.

Just then, Robert got to the car and apologized for taking so long. We had a nice drive back into Missouri to the west side where the suburbs of St. Louis are. It seemed like the conversation was mostly Rob and I giving our friend trouble. "Does he still do that 'I can get you where you want to go' stuff?" he asked.

I started laughing, "Yep," I said. "I didn't know he had a playbook."

"Oh yeah. Some days it's flat-out torture," he continued. "If he didn't volunteer to give me a break covering expenses while I was learning, I don't think I would have put up with it. What gutter did he find you in?"

"I can see that you're still learning yourself," Matt chimed in. Robert looked puzzled as Matt gave him his signature shit-eating grin. "He is an over-the-road truck driver." Robert now seemed even more puzzled and it got quiet for a second. "Robert understands that, at some point, in order to grow further, humility is required. A lot of my students, and his I would suspect, therefore come from much more financially modest places, oftentimes destitute. His line of logic is that someone who is doing well financially may have a more difficult time reaching the level of humility required to put up with the work necessary for growth.

What he doesn't understand is while money can afford one the luxury of peace of mind financially, there are many other ways the mind can torture itself."

I was intrigued by that and wanted to discuss it further, but we had reached the restaurant, and I was anxious to get out of the car. "Shish KeRob's," I read aloud.

"No more serving food out of the back of a van for me. Still love cooking, though, but never on Sundays," he proclaimed with a smile.

The place was amazing. It had a really cool ambience about it. There were little pretend fire pits placed strategically on half-walls and cutouts. There were trendy but comfortable-looking booths and tables broken up in a way that made the seating areas seem more private. The layout had a lot of corners with diamond patterns, but in a way that seemed more welcoming than a lot of other contemporary styles. Robert could tell I was impressed.

"So?" he questioned.

"Nice!" I enthusiastically replied. "You own this place?"

"Yep, I had a feng shui expert help me with the design," he explained. "This is my favorite location and if I open any others, I think I'll use this one as the basis for the layout. Nice, huh?" he repeated.

"I'll say, and it doesn't look like you lost much in the way of seating, arranging it like this, either," I added.

"No," he said, surprised that I would notice something like that.

"I have an eye for aesthetics and am very practical," I said. "This place welcomes me on both levels. The only drawback I can see is that your customers might have a tendency to linger. You have other locations?.

"Yeah, two others. I'm not sure I want to branch out any further because I'm too busy as it is, but I keep getting offers of doing a franchise and things like that because of the success I've had. I've also had a few buyout offers that were more money than I ever thought a guy like me could be worth, but I love cooking for people. It brings me joy that they appreciate my food."

As soon as we arrived, the hostess had gone to get the manager, and he greeted us with a warm smile as he was introduced, and seated us at a table. After we placed our drink orders, Robert instructed the manager to give our friend a tour of the kitchen and show him how they prepared and cooked the food, allowing him an all-access pass saying he had free reign to do whatever he liked. That was all the encouragement Matt needed and they were gone.

"If I know him, he'll be cooking our dinner tonight," he said, laughing. "So how are you doing?"

"I'm doing good," I replied. It was a standard answer. I wasn't quite sure what he meant, so I figured if he didn't go into detail I would leave it at that.

"Has he driven you crazy yet?" he asked.

"No," I drew out, seeming puzzled.

"He will. I just wanted you to know that it's worth it." After saying that, his smile left and he got rather serious, "I owe everything to that man. You have no idea the magnitude of which he can change your life."

"Yeah, it seems like mostly financially. He's a millionaire, and you seem to be doing real well," I added.

"I couldn't care less about that stuff. It doesn't mean anything," he explained. "It's just an outward reflection of the joy within."

"I don't know about all that," I replied, unconvinced. "I think it's much easier to not be concerned about money when you have plenty of it, and as far as joy is concerned, I've seen some pretty unhappy rich people." Robert smiled that big, familiar, "My, we have much to learn"–smile I was too used to seeing, but not from him.

"Not you too," I said. "Why do you guys look at me as if I'm stupid? You know, I think my viewpoint is fairly normal."

"Normal's not very fun, is it? I mean, it has its moments, but wouldn't you prefer extraordinary?" he asked, somewhat rhetorically. "Speaking of extraordinary," he said with a cocky grin, picking up my menu and handing it to me, "I'm going to have to let you look over the menu so we can eat soon."

I looked over the menu. It seemed to basically have only two things, shish kebabs (or rather shish keRobs) and rice. There were twenty different kebabs to choose from, ten that were always on the menu and ten that alternated; two kinds of beans; and five kinds of rice. I didn't see that any that seemed objectionable, so I told him to choose the kebabs for me but that I wanted the saffron rice. He asked me what salad dressing I wanted for the salad and I replied, "House." I always replied house if they had one, even before knowing what it was. I like to see what may come and my palate is not usually offended by any of them.

"Very well, I'll see if our friend wants to prepare it for us, under my chef's direction, of course," he said and headed to the kitchen.

When he returned, I asked him how he came up with the theme for the restaurant. "Well, I love cooking on a grill, and these days people are so health conscious that it just makes sense to offer something relatively healthy. Vegetarians can enjoy having a choice of veggie kebabs with rice and beans. Of course, our meats are very lean and are grilled. Some of the marinades, sauces and rubs are high in sugar and salt, but it's still relatively healthy and can be ordered plain. But the most important thing about this type of menu is that, even though it's healthy, there's no sacrificing flavor. There are other technical benefits as well, like streamlining the kitchen, ordering and storing food, minimizing costs, etc."

"Sounds smart," I commented.

"Smart and delicious," he said. "Presentation is beautiful as well. I'd like to delve into finance a bit more if you want."

"About the restaurant?" I asked.

"No, about obtaining wealth," he said.

"Yeah, I am curious about that outward expression comment. It seems a bit conceited to me when rich people act like they don't care about money … no offense," I said with the sound of frustration in my voice. "If they don't care about money, then why don't they just give it all to me?"

He laughed and replied, "It's not like that. It's about the feeling of being wealthy."

"I'm not feeling very wealthy right now," I said jokingly.

"And so you are not wealthy," he replied as if it were a logical answer to a simple equation.

"I'm not wealthy because I'm not making enough money to be wealthy," I said.

"No, you're not making enough money to be wealthy because you don't feel wealthy," he replied while watching my look of confusion grow.

"I'm dying for a conversation not muddled in riddles," I said, slumping back.

He seemed to become a bit more sympathetic at that and leaned in a little towards me. "Let me explain it to you like this. A long time ago, I had a dream. In this dream I was extremely wealthy. When I woke up, what do you think I wanted to do?" he asked.

"I don't know, become rich?" I answered, still lingering in my frustration.

"No," he answered. "I wanted to go back to the sleep so I could get back to the dream. The reason I wanted to go back was to experience the feeling of being rich again. Think about it. I woke up and came to the realization that I was still the same financially as I had been and, of course, I knew the money in the dream wasn't real, so why else would I want to go back?" Even though the question was rhetorical, he paused for a moment. "I didn't care that it wasn't real. I wanted that feeling back. Once you've created the feeling of being wealthy in your life, actually being wealthy is no longer a concern."

"But you are," I said, trying to make clear to him that he had not yet connected the dots for me.

"Yes, I am. When you are in harmony with something on a level of thought, God – or as Matt says, 'the universe' – causes the physical to be a match with it. Because I have felt wealthy for a while now, I am wealthy. I couldn't care less about the money, though, because all I really care about is the feeling I get from it," he explained.

"Yeah, but you can't buy something with a feeling," I retorted.

"Okay," he said. "Name something extravagant you can't buy without money."

"I don't know, a yacht," I replied unenthusiastically. It was the first thing that popped into my head.

"If I can experience the feelings of owning the yacht, what do I need the yacht for?" he asked.

"Taking it out for a spin, enjoying it on the water in the sun, having parties on it. I could go on," I said in a smart-ass but friendly way.

"I can experience all of those feelings," he stated very matter-of-factly, "and if I do it long enough, it will become my reality. You can experience any reality you like, even before you physically experience it, just like I did in the dream. It takes practice and repetition. Doing this also allows you to better determine exactly what experiences you want to have by giving you a preview of what it would be like to have it. Then, as you do it repetitively, it either proves to be something in harmony with who you truly are and it becomes a physical reality or you lose interest and it fades."

"So what about all of the unhappy rich people?" I asked.

"That has to do with the opposite, being reactionary," he paused as if he was wrestling with something.

"I thought it had to do with feelings?" I asked, puzzled.

"Your thoughts cause your feelings," he replied. "Look, I don't want get into it too much because I don't want to disrupt Matt's training with you, but when you do not direct your thoughts, they default to your reactions to your circumstances and events. If one was to grow up in an affluent home, one might view the financial future optimistically, and having one's thoughts dwell in that realm enables their future to be so. Someone who grew up in a financially optimistic but emotionally distraught household might fit your scenario. This is why I preach in my old neighborhood. When the children there see the future in their parents' eyes, it looks bleak, sometimes both financially and emotionally. If I can break that cycle for just some of them, I've given them a gift as great as your friend has given me."

Just then, Matt arrived with salads and sat down with us.

"We were just talking about you," Robert said. "Did you enjoy the kitchen?"

"Very impressive. I had so much fun in there. Your staff is so kind," he said.

We ate our salads while Matt described what he had prepared for us. He explained that two of the kebabs were just vegetables. One was marinated in Italian dressing, and the other was plain with an herbal medley thrown on just before cooking, along with coarse salt and pepper.

There were three meat varieties we would try as well. One was called Sticky Chicken. A chicken breast was filleted and cut into strips so that it was thin enough to cook quickly, and when one side was done, it was flipped and brushed with a barbecue sauce that had canned mandarin oranges added (with the light syrup) and a little extra sugar or brown sugar. Then it's flipped again and brushed again. The sugary sauce quickly caramelizes and is then seasoned with lemon pepper. The steak dinner, as it was called, had medium-rare steak, sautéed onions and mushrooms. The mushrooms and onions were sautéed prior to being grilled, so that they would be done without overcooking the steak and they wouldn't be too dry. It was brushed with steak sauce, and though the meat was salt-and-peppered before cooking, fresh cracked pepper was added at the end.

The Mad Hawaiian was simply cubed ham, pineapple, and maraschino cherries. When it was finished cooking, it was covered in soy sauce and lightly dusted with onion powder. I was glad the food arrived by the time he had described it all because I was dying to try it.

The food was unbelievably good. I understood the success he had with this restaurant with the first bite. Not only were the kebabs amazing, I had never had such good rice before. I think the sound and expressions on my face let them know how I felt about it. Robert looked to Matt and said, "Let me know if you ever want a job as the chef in one of my restaurants. This is superb."

"It's a superb representation of your work," he replied. "I didn't deviate from the recipe. I'm not even sure your staff would have let me. They really know their stuff."

"I only hire people who want to share in my vision. My vision is to make people so happy about their dining experience that they want to come back every time. My staff takes it almost as personally as I do when someone has an unpleasant experience. Luckily, it doesn't happen very often."

"I won't be back," I said.

"Really, why?" Robert asked, very puzzled.

"No truck parking," I said with a smart-ass grin that let him know I was kidding him.

I then added, "Actually, that's not true. For this, I would take a cab." His look of concern had turned to a smile of someone who had been had.

"All kidding aside, though," I continued, "this truly is phenomenal and I hope you do branch out so that I can have it in other parts of the country as well."

When we finished the meal, all I could think about was taking a nap and was kind of glad Robert had plans for the afternoon. He did give us a ride back to the hotel, though, and even drove us by my truck so I could check on it.

Robert and Matt were catching up with each other the whole way back, which was fine with me because it was a struggle to hear them from the backseat anyway.

When we arrived at the hotel, I thanked him for the meal and again expressed how wonderful the food and his restaurant were. I then went up to the room while they were saying their goodbyes. I went straight to the bed and hoped Matt wouldn't wake me when he came in.

When I finally stirred from my slumber, I found Matt watching another stock market news program. I told him I was going to the hot tub and asked him if he wanted to join me. He declined, saying he was doing research and I didn't feel bad about it. I needed to do some reflecting about all that had gone on. I wondered if maybe Matt realized that. It didn't matter, I wanted to relax and try to get this stuff straight in my head.

143

Tomorrow, I would be on the road again and it would be business as usual.

Relaxing in the hot water was just what I needed. I think my body had tension in it from all this heady stuff, if that's even possible. I mean, how did this guy go from living in his van to being so successful and what did it have to do with peace of mind? Why did my new friend choose to wander the country helping people when he could do anything he wanted? Can you really create a reality or did they just psych themselves into doing what was necessary to achieve their goals? Was it the same? I sighed a sigh of frustration and lowered my body into the water until my head was submerged. Though it was really hot, it felt good to have my head enveloped in the water, the sounds of the hot tub drowning out my thoughts. Maybe that's all I needed because I felt more at ease after that. I remembered Matt doing that "ah" thing and looked around to make sure no one was around so I could try it out. Once I was sure I was alone, I said to myself that my intention was to receive clarity and peace.

I then started chanting the "ah" sound as I had heard him do. It made a really cool sound in the pool room. I did it a few times, trying to do it as I had heard it. I found it very relaxing but didn't have any intense feelings or anything. Maybe I was doing it wrong. Finding no measurable results, I quickly became discouraged and gave up, deciding just to enjoy the relaxing water. After a minute or so, though, I found myself wanting to do it again, so I did. I don't know why exactly, it just felt good. After a while, though, I got bored with it and jumped in the pool to cool down.

Chapter 9

Double Take

Getting back to the room, I found Matt napping. After a quick shower, I went straight to the computer. I found a sticky note on it that read, "Begin answering any question you feel inspired to, whether it's related to judgment or not." So I did. This was much more fun. I felt I knew enough that I could help people with other things, and I liked answering opinion questions. I found myself once again engrossed in the website. Questions like, "If God had a dog, what would his name be?" are just plain fun to answer. I was just as puzzled, though, about the same questions other people were asking. Over and over I read, "What is the meaning of life?" in one form or another.

Someone asked the question, "If a Buddhist monk walked into a pizza place, do you think he would ask them to make him one with everything?" This reminded me that I was starting to get hungry again and I started perusing the room service menu. I hadn't quite decided what I might like when I heard the shower turn on in Matt's room, so I figured I'd wait till he came out. When he did, he was once again dressed in his suit.

"Let's go out to eat tonight," he suggested. "There's a great place right around the corner, and it will give us an opportunity to wear our suits one last time."

"I like the idea of it being the last time," I said. "I guess I do look good in a suit," I warmed up. "All right," I said finally, relenting. I really didn't have the desire to go out, but I didn't get the opportunity to do it very often because it's not much fun doing it alone, so I quickly psyched myself into the idea and headed into my room to get dressed. When I came out, the first words out of my mouth were, "Suit and tie, huh?

He could hear the concern by the tone in my voice and said, "Don't worry, sport, I'm buying," and then added, "I'll let you get the tip," with a smug grin.

"Here's a tip you'll appreciate, buy low, sell high," I said, giving it back to him.

The place was really classy. Matt had found this place via the suggestion of the concierge on his previous stay. I whispered to him that we might need reservations but the maître d' very excitedly greeted us with a smile, asking Matt how he had been. My friend seemed to have this effect on people wherever he went. Apparently, he had the hotel make the reservations for him earlier. The dining room was very elegantly done in a black-and-white theme; the curtains were black with white drapes, the tablecloths were white with black cloth napkins, and there was a glossy, black grand piano in the center of the back wall on a white raised platform. I was a bit overwhelmed and hoped I would not do anything that would embarrass myself, but I played it off as best I could.

Matt, however, always seemed at ease and ordered us some wine. I don't like wine at all, except for some of the sweeter Moscatos, but I resolved to sip some slowly anyway, drinking mostly water. The menu items seemed delicious yet limited. I guess concentrating one's efforts within a narrow field is better than scattering one's attention on too many endeavors. I'm sure Matt would have something to say about that, but right now I didn't want to hear it, and I thought it might make me appear further out of my element. After a brief description of the daily special I was sold, and after ordering, I excused myself to the restroom.

Once again, this was another opportunity to stir my anxiousness, as there was an attendant. I never liked the idea of bathroom attendants. The thought of someone monitoring the bathroom made me very uncomfortable. Then I had to decide if I was supposed to tip for the privilege of peeing. While I was walking to the sink, I heard the piano starting to play. Shortly thereafter it was accompanied by the most beautiful voice I had ever heard. I immediately relaxed, and felt so good I put a dollar on the tip plate. Walking back to the table, I noticed that my minor anxiety had vanished, and everything felt right. I looked over at the woman who had such an angelic voice and my heart began to race. It was the woman who handed me the note at the truck stop. I had a hard time finding my way back to the table and almost walked right by it because I was enthralled with her performance. I wondered why no one else seemed to be paying much attention to her. When I got back to the table, I immediately said, "Do you know who that is?"

"Yeah," he answered casually.

"Wait a minute. Did you know she was going to be here?" I asked.

"No," he replied.

After a few more seconds of being enchanted and distracted by her, I added, "You do know that she's the girl from the truck stop, right, the one who I embarrassed myself in front of?"

"Yeahhh," he dragged out, as if I was completely overreacting.

I struggled with whether I should continue to try to help Matt understand what an amazing coincidence this was or to engulf myself in the heavenly experience that was before me. I could no longer struggle against the hypnotic music that no one else seemed able to hear. Our salads arrived but I hardly noticed as Matt was indulging in his. In fact, I was out of it until the main course arrived. The only reason I came out of my trance for that was our waiter's concern for my not eating the salad. All I could manage was a simple no—repeating it twice—to his question about anything being wrong with it. Matt managed to explain that I was just caught up in the entertainment and to leave it for when I came back to planet earth. They shared a chuckle over it, which stirred me out of my hypnotic state long enough to realize it would be very awkward if I didn't eat soon.

I decided that it was better to eat the main course first or else it would get cold. I was on sensory overload as I ate my meal. I don't know exactly what it was. I wanted to try something different and I heard the words "colossal lump crab," some sort of sauce that sounded French, and "lemon." There was more to it than that, and if I hadn't been so self-conscious I would have paid closer attention. I was right in assuming that I would like it, though. All I know is that the combination of what I was seeing, hearing and tasting put me in a state of ecstasy. Matt just smiled at it all. I believe that he, too, enjoyed sharing experiences with others and was getting more enjoyment from my amusement than the experience itself. He didn't want to detract from my enjoyment so he kept quiet as we sat enjoying it all.

After we had eaten the main course, the waiter explained our dessert choices. Again, we went with the special of the day, peaches flambé. The waiter explained that the chef had found some exceptional peaches at the market that day, so we were sold.

The waiter and Matt seemed to share amusement over my being so distracted. I barely noticed the usual show the waiter was putting on that accompanies flambé. It is part of the experience and part of what you're paying for, but it was wasted on me, for I never tired of watching her. Dessert was really good, and though I had a glass of wine in front of me that I never touched, with the wonderful experience I was having, I didn't want to spoil it, so when Matt questioned me about it, I offered it to him.

It wasn't until my angel quit playing that I agreed to leave, and on the walk back, I expressed my concern that I might not ever see her again. "Maybe I should go back and see if I can find out who she is at least," I said.

"You'll be fine," he said, continuing to walk.

"How can you be so callous?" I asked.

"I'm not," he replied.

"I'm not convinced you'd be so cavalier about it if you were the one interested," I complained.

"Look, you are in the beginning stages of creating a reality worthy of your divine nature. This means that things will be starting to fall into place soon. The universe delights in bringing us joy, and when we set a course for our desire, often they start chasing us. If she is meant to be in your future, it will be," he explained.

"That's one of the questions that keeps popping up on that answer website. So everything does happen for a reason?" I asked.

"Yes, but it's all based on thought, not necessarily one's best interest. It's not until you start directing your thoughts that a desired result will be inevitable. People who say everything happens for a reason often have no clue that they are the ones determining the reason," he said.

"So my girl back there," I paused, waiting for him to fill in the blanks for me. When he didn't, I continued excitedly, "I can make her my desired reality?"

"No," he said.

I walked more briskly to stand in front of him, blocking his path, and stopped. "Look, I get that you're doing this whole song-and-dance thing to keep me on my toes, but I need you to be serious for a minute," I stated seriously.

He could tell this was very important to me, so he explained further, "You can't create someone else's reality. In relationships, you must be a match. They have to be in harmony with you as much as you are with them or it is doomed for failure. Asking the universe to hook you up with a specific person is like asking it to give you something you will not like."

Seeing the disappointment on my face, he added, "You tell the universe your desires and it grants you them—you know, 'your wish is my command,' so to speak. But you have to let it choose things that are in harmony with your frequencies. It knows the best and most harmonious way to bring you your desires. Therefore, you tell it what you desire in a friend and lover and it brings them to you."

I slumped down in disappointment and we started walking again. "So, do you want the good news?" he asked.

With this new information Matt had given me, my disappointment was overwhelming and I wasn't sure he could give me any that would help at all. "What?" I sighed.

"When it comes to the universe, there are no limitations of time," he said, smiling.

"Yeah, yeah. One day I'll be outrageously happy with someone," I said, the disappointment still lingering in my voice.

He chuckled, which ordinarily would have pissed me off, but I was too sad to get angry. "No," he said, stopping me in my tracks this time. "It can be retroactive."

I stood there looking confused for a moment, and then I realized what he had meant. "You mean—" I started to say.

"You may be beginning to become a match vibrationally to a desire you have not yet made known," he explained. After a pause he added, "I don't know, she's popped up in your life twice and you are obviously smitten."

My face lit up again. "Maybe we should go back," I said excitedly.

"No, she is a distraction you don't need right now," he said. "Besides, things aren't in alignment with her or you would probably be walking with her right now." He could see the look of disappointment return and added, "This is where faith comes in. When you make a declaration of intent to the universe, you must have faith that it not only hears you but will grant you your desires. It always knows what's best. Take your crush back there…"

"I'd hardly call her a crush," I corrected, though not quite believing it myself.

"Whatever," he dismissed. "She might be married, maybe even happily so. Or maybe she's married and not happy in her marriage, but it will be another two years before she's emotionally available. Whether or not she's the girl for your needs is to be determined by the universe, not you. You will always be happier with the choices it makes for you. You ask for what you want by way of consciously directing your thoughts and attaching emotion to them, and then you let it be decided for you that which will draw out the most of the emotion you seek. What most people don't understand is that it is the underlying emotion of something that they are seeking, not the actual thing. This is why when you ask, it is not instantaneous. You have to experience the emotions before you receive in order to determine if it is something you truly want. As you experience the emotions of it daily, it either continues to resonate in your heart or it fades as your focus shifts to something else. When you become an emotional match to something," he added with emphasis, "or someone, it chases after you. Well, I don't mean literally, of course. I just mean that everything falls into place."

"Yeah," I said with a sigh. "That's what Robert said, too, more or less."

"So then how about we shift your current focus on lack to that of gratitude. Since what you focus on expands and right now you are focused on lack, tell me what you're grateful for," he suggested.

I threw him a look that let him know I wasn't pleased with the idea, but it didn't seem to faze him, so I said, "I'm grateful you paid for dinner, thank you." Then I started remembering how wonderful it was and added, "I'm grateful for the whole experience. I'm grateful just to have company right now. I'm grateful not to be cramped up in that damn truck..." I continued the rest of the way like that. It seemed I did have a lot to be grateful for and I felt silly about my little pity party earlier. I was starting to feel really good.

I got on the computer to dole out some more advice and noticed that Matt had left his account on the answer site up. I decided to sneak a peek at one of his answers. The question was, "How can I be happy?" His answer was as follows:

Emotions are brought to us by our subconscious mind, based solely on our thoughts. In fact, our entire reality is created by our thoughts. Our thoughts are received by our subconscious, which, in turn, causes us to do things (subconsciously) that create a reality congruent with them. Our predominant thoughts become habitual, which literally hardwires the neurons in our brains so that they form what is called a neural net. If we want to create a new reality, it is necessary to change our habitual thought patterns so that the neural net becomes rewired.

Most of us derive our thoughts from the input of our circumstances and experiences. When we operate from that dynamic, we are destined to live a life that reflects our current reality. The wonderful thing about the human mind is that we cannot only change what we experience to a large degree; we can direct our thoughts so that they are congruent with the reality we would like to experience. In doing this, we shift our thoughts from reactionary to visionary.

The first thing necessary to start creating a reality you desire is to free yourself from judgment. This not only enables you to feel you deserve to have the reality you desire; it keeps you from judging your desires, and it is these very desires that will lead you not only to that which brings you the greatest joy in life, but also will be the most beneficial to others as well. Affirmations are one of the most powerful ways to do this and also one of the practices that are most frequently done incorrectly. Not only do affirmations have to be done in the present tense (as if already achieved) and in the positive, but the emotions of it already being your reality must be experienced. This is similar to what great actors and actresses do when they get "into character." They also have to be habitual, so must be done at least once daily. The affirmation for judgment needs to be said to yourself but about other people. By saying the phrase, "You are *perfect and beautiful," to yourself (not aloud) about random people, it not only frees yourself from judgment of others but yourself as well.*

Once you have freed yourself of judgment, you can use this technique to start creating other realities you desire. Some good general affirmations are, "My thoughts are in line with my desires," "My happiness grows greater by the day," or, "I believe that anything is possible." Visualization, creativity and guided meditation are other good ways to bring about your reality. The same rules apply to those methods as affirmations. The basic idea is to experience for a few minutes every day the reality you wish to create and the emotions you would have if it were your current reality.

Another great thing that helps to shift your thought process is to start a gratitude journal. By focusing on what you lack in life, you bring about more that causes you to feel that way. By focusing on what you are grateful for, you bring about more to be grateful for. Just write down one thing you are grateful for every day and focus on the list while feeling the gratitude for a minute. After a week, date it and start over.

When you begin changing your thinking to be in line with your desires, your old way of thinking will begin to concern you because it is so prominent and out of line with the reality you're trying to create. Don't panic. Whatever you think about with emotion, you bring about, so if you are worried about it or try to fight it, it will just become more prominent. Like a gardener, you are planting seeds and watering them daily. It will take time to bear fruit.

You may at times find yourself a bit despondent as well. This is because your body is adjusting to the new emotional peptides your brain is sending it. Honor your feelings but remind your body that you are doing this for its best interest, and continue the techniques so that they become habitual.

Change your input. Read inspirational material about someone who has mastered a reality you would like to emulate. Watch inspiring movies and uplifting television. Limit input incongruent with your desired reality.

It is essential to have a good understanding of how the mind works so that it can start working for you instead of against you. Some people will spend their whole lives running around in circles, wondering why they can't get anywhere in life. Our minds require that we set a destination for ourselves so that it knows where to take us. After declaring our destination, it is simply a matter of letting go and going with the flow of the universe. I wish you well, and I hope that you end up exactly where you want to go.

Chapter 10

Back to Work

The next day I awoke and called dispatch. We were showered, packed and off to the lobby quickly. Matt had made arrangements for the suits to be donated. I wasn't quite sure if they would make it to the local Goodwill or if they were going to be the property of whoever he gave them to, but I figured either way, they wouldn't be wasted. While we grabbed some bagels and coffee on the way out, the hotel was kind enough to shuttle us to my truck.

We didn't have to load far from where the church we had attended was. In fact, it was a scrap metal place just down the street from it. When we got there, we had to unhook from the trailer so they could have one of their trucks take it around back to load. This is somewhat unusual, but some places with limited space find that inexperienced drivers cause so much damage that it's just easier to do it themselves. Generally, they have a much shorter truck, which makes it easier for them anyway. This may have been the case here, but I suspect it may also be due to all the scrap metal doing damage to tires.

As we sat there, Matt had me add to my gratitude list and concentrate on it. He then had me do something different.

"Write down everything that frustrates you in life right now," he said. So I started writing. As I did, I realized that it all seemed to revolve around my job. It actually starts with the fact that the pay for truck drivers is completely out of line with the rest of the country. We generally get paid by the mile but those who drive locally are often paid by the hour. Getting paid hourly, you would think that like everyone else, after a forty-hour workweek, we would get time and a half. While some employers abide by that, it's not required by law … we're exempt and I have worked for companies that don't.

Getting paid by the mile can be very frustrating as well. We don't get paid for the actual miles we drive; we get paid by a guide. Generally, it is five to ten percent fewer miles than we actually have to drive. It can be even less than that because of the route we have to take due to the restricted roads for trucks. Anything that delays us is on us. If we break down, we don't get paid for it. If it takes four hours at the shipper, we don't get paid for it. If we sit in traffic for an hour, we don't get paid for it. If the department of transportation wants to inspect our truck for an hour, we don't get paid for it. In fact, if they find anything wrong we have to pay for it, at least the fines involved.

The mere procedure of getting inspected is harassment in and of itself. The percentage of trucks that get into an accident is far less than the percentage of cars, yet cars do not get pulled over for random inspections.

The rest of the list went on like that and I found myself getting pissed. I finally stopped because I was so aggravated at what I saw as complete injustice. Matt looked over at me and said, "Had enough yet?"

"Yeah," I said emphatically, the frustration obvious in my tone.

"As you can see, when we focus on that which we don't like, we experience the emotions of what we don't like. They become stronger the more we concentrate on them," he started to explain.

"So this is like the guy at the doctor who said every time he moves his arm like this, it hurts, and the doctor tells him not to move his arm like that?" I said in frustration.

"A little bit, yeah," he replied. "Only you don't have to move your arm like that in order to enjoy a full life."

"So I just ignore things that make me feel bad?" I asked.

"No," he replied. "Take away their power."

"My ignoring this list of aggravations will not cause them to disappear. I will still be subject to them from time to time," I explained.

"Ignoring them might not, but taking their power away by not only stealing their focus but also directing your thoughts elsewhere will," he said matter-of-factly.

"So the rules that apply to everybody else will somehow no longer apply to me," I said as if pointing out the flaw in his logic.

"Exactly," he said very contently. "You will float above them." He waited for a moment to let this sink in. He could tell I was struggling with this. "You said it better than I could have. The same rules that apply to everyone else will no longer apply to you. Your frequency will no longer be a match."

I sat there for a minute. I didn't want to try to debate it further and I wondered if it was true. The rules of life didn't seem to apply to him at all, and Robert also seemed to be an exception to the rules of life. This was too much for me to take into my belief system just on his word, though, so I resolved just to observe how things played out to see if they rang true. Sometimes I was starving for his teachings and sometimes I felt like I had spent too much time in the sun when he was around, so I was glad to find out that my load was ready and we could pick up the trailer from their scales. When hauling scrap, the trailer is often weighed before and after being loaded, as it is generally sold by the pound. Most of the time it is done both at the shipper and the receiver. After getting our bills (bills of lading), we were off.

"Okay, it's time to start training again," he said, grinning from ear to ear.

"Did we ever really stop?" I replied.

"You might not have stopped learning but we took a break from training and it's time to get back," he explained. "We have a whole new set of proclamations. Let's start with 'I have complete faith in the universe,'" he said.

"I have complete faith in the universe," I said overly enthusiastically.

"Sarcasm is never helpful even in jest when it comes to this, you know," he explained.

"All right," I relented and said it as if it were already true, as he had taught me. After my third time he gave me the next one. The phrases he used were like the general ones I had read in his answer: things like "I create my reality in the fashion that I desire," "Every day my intelligence and wisdom gets greater," and "I stay highly motivated to create the reality I desire." This went on for a few minutes and then he was quiet.

"That's it?" I asked.

"No," he replied, "but that is all the affirmations we are doing this morning. Now we are going to do the 'ah' meditation. Simply concentrate on the proclamations you've just made and say the 'ah' sound and hold it for a while. Don't worry about giving it your full attention; you can still pay attention to your driving. Just relax and let your thoughts go as you release your intent. Give yourself a few seconds between each one."

I did this for a few minutes and then he said it was enough. "Now you've already spent some time this morning looking at the things you don't like about your life," he said. "These are the things that will no longer be a part of your future because you are going to release them."

"How am I going to do that?" I asked excitedly.

"By giving your attention to something else," he explained. "I need you to spend the day focusing on the things about your life that you are grateful for."

"So my gratitude list is going to expand, huh?" I asked.

"No, it will still be one thing a day," he replied. "That is merely an exercise to cause your gratitude to become habitual. This is an exercise for you to see just how much you have to be grateful for. You will find that as you spend time focusing on gratitude, it feeds on itself. Eventually, you will become amazed at how wonderful your life already is."

"And this will somehow nullify the list of things I don't like?" I asked

"It won't nullify the list. But it will take away its power," he explained. "Think of it like your GPS. When you select a destination, it feeds you a series of right and left turns that you need to make in order to get there. Your mind works in a similar way. When you select a destination by concentrating your thoughts on your desires, your subconscious starts causing you to do things that will lead you to them. When you continually focus your thoughts on where you currently are, you stay where you are. Unlike your GPS, though, you can give your mind vague commands like the ones we did this morning or a specific destination. Both the general and the specific will lead you from an undesired place, but the specific destination will lead you to your bliss. Your specific destination can only be determined by you and is a process, one which we will be covering how to do later."

I said, a little peeved, "You say it will take away its power, but I don't understand how that could change the pay system in the trucking industry to one that I think is fair, for instance,"

I continued, "You make all this sound like the universe will somehow bend the rules for me and my reality will be different than everyone else's. I don't see how this can work."

"Your reality is different than everyone else's," he said, pausing for effect.

Before he could continue, I interjected, "So you actually do think that they will change the pay system just for me?"

He smiled. I think he knew how his smile melted my defenses, and he was using it to do just that. "I don't know how your reality will shift so that this is no longer an issue. Maybe you will simply become at peace with it. Maybe you will work to have it changed. Maybe you will change jobs or even professions. These things are determined by your subconscious in conjunction with the universe. Your reality will change, not necessarily shared reality."

"Shared reality?" I queried.

"When a tree falls in the woods does it make a sound?" he asked.

"Of course," I replied.

"How do you know?" he continued.

"Just because no one is there doesn't mean that it doesn't make a sound," I said as if it was obvious.

"You're actually right but I don't think you understand why. When I mentioned that all life is sacred, I meant it. It is not only sacred but we are connected with it. Just because we are not there to hear a tree falling in the woods, life is. Animals can hear it and even insects and plants experience sound on some level. It's well-documented that plants actually have different growth patterns based on the music they are subjected to. There's even a guy in Japan who's measured reactions of water based on exposure to words and music. He does it by flash-freezing it shortly after exposing it to words, music or prayers and viewing the crystal formations under a microscope.

"So we now have a way to recognize that even water is affected in some way by this connection or shared reality," Matt went on to explain. "You don't have to walk on water to get to the other side of the lake. Someone with a boat might present himself or you might be led to a clear and direct path around it. Of course, that doesn't mean walking on water is impossible, but that's generally too far outside our belief systems, and as I have taught you, anything you think is impossible, is."

"So how do I get my mind wrapped around the concept that the rules everyone else lives by don't apply to me?" I asked. "It sounds like I have to have almost as much faith to believe that as I do that I can walk on water."

"The same way you went about believing you are perfect just as you are," he replied. "Anything you desire requires only that you shift your thinking so that it is in line with it. When your emotions become in harmony, more often than not, it will become your reality."

"So I could use this method to walk on water?" I asked. "That would be really cool," I said, grinning at the fact that it might be possible.

"I think you have yet to determine what your desired reality is, but it's highly unlikely that it includes walking on water," he stated, looking at me as if he were trying to see over an imaginary pair of glasses. "If walking on water is a requirement for you to create a reality congruent with your true nature, which is a state of bliss, you will be able to walk across it with ease."

I quietly growled at this. "Why can't this be simpler? Why can't I just instantly get the life I want?" I asked in frustration, knowing that I was oversimplifying.

"It is easy," he said. He saw the disagreement in my eyes and added, "You've just been doing it the wrong way for so long that we have to retrain your brain. I don't have to work at this at all. I've been doing this so long that everything happens in my life with ease. You are the one fighting the flow of the universe, my friend.

I'm just waiting for you to let go of the belief system that's weighing you down so that I can teach you how to swim with the current."

"Yeah, I've got a question about that," I said. "It's one that's popped up on that answer website a couple of times."

"Okay, shoot," he said.

"Shouldn't life be lived for others?" I asked and then proceeded to clarify. "I mean, Mother Teresa said that a life not lived for others is a life not lived or something like that. Einstein had a similar quote I believe. I know that you and Robert help people, but what you're telling me is to move toward my desires and my desired reality. What if my reality isn't helpful to anyone but myself?"

He smiled really big at this. He was almost beaming as he said, "That is one of the most beautiful designs of the universe. When you create a reality congruent with your desires, it is congruent with divinity. Whether your desired reality helps people directly, like a doctor or a preacher, for instance, or less directly, like a carpenter or a businessman, you're the most helpful to others when you have the most passion for it. Mother Teresa had a passion for helping others, so her statement is correct about her reality as well as the reality of many others, including myself, I might add."

"All right, but what about the money?" I asked.

"You're really hung up on this money thing, aren't you?" he asked rhetorically. "You're going to have to work on judgment for a bit longer as far as money is concerned, I think. You benefit others the most when you not only follow your bliss but you are blissful. Being blissful includes abundance in all aspects of life. My guess is that because you are so hung up on this, you desire it much more than you are willing to admit and judge yourself as being wrong for it."

"What about altruism, though?" I said, ignoring his observation about me being hung up on money. "I've always thought that putting others first is for the highest good."

"So you want to play God?" he asked.

I slid my hand over my forehead and past my hair. I was beginning to hate it when he did that, so I mentioned it: "You know, I hate it when you do that." I then answered his question, "Of course not."

"Who, then, gets to decide what the highest good for someone else is?" he asked, pausing for my obvious realization that it was something I hadn't pondered. "The Nazi party is an example of altruism taken to its extreme on a very large scale, but how about we just address it on a very small scale, say, a homeless man begging for change on the street? Do you know what's in his best interest? Is it good to give him money, knowing that it could very well contribute to the very thing that brought him where he is? Do you buy him a sandwich? Do you try to get him help? How do you determine what is in his best interest? Living life for the best interest of others just adds one more person to the pile that needs help. We are ordained with the blessing of free will; trying to impose our will on others leads to disharmony."

I thought about this for a moment. This was something I hadn't considered in that dichotomy. I had gone back and forth on it. Sometimes, I gave a homeless person money, sometimes not. I have offered to buy a few beggars a meal so they would not spend the money on alcohol or drugs and even got turned down a couple of times on that offer. Even though I have tried to come up with the solution as to how I could best help them, none of the ways seemed very helpful. Then I remembered that he had mentioned giving half the proceeds of the sale of his stuff to charity. "What about charity?" I asked.

"What about it?" he replied.

"You give money to charity, do you not? I mean, you mentioned how you did it at least once," I pointed out.

"Yes. I regularly give to charity," he replied. "One of the wonderful things about living life in abundance is that you get to pass on the overflow. I love helping others."

"Is that not altruism in its most tangible form?" I asked, seeing this as a clear contradiction.

He sighed. It was a sigh of disappointment. I knew that because I was used to it. He noticed by my reaction that I had taken it personally. "I'm sorry. I'm not actually frustrated with you in this matter; it's just that your sentiment is shared by so many these days," he said, taking a moment to collect his thoughts for an answer. "I give to the charities that are most in line with my desired reality. If I want to give to a charity that sends money to a third-world country to help the children of that country, that is an expression of my desire. If I give to a charity that strictly helps the people in my community, that is an expression of my desire. Everything I do, I do for myself."

"Yeah, but you're an exception to the rule," I countered. "Most people aren't like you, though. You live in a world all your own."

"We all live in a world all our own," he said with a smile.

"You know what I mean," I said, a bit frustrated. "There are plenty of greedy rich people out there, that don't give a dime to charity or at least a dime more than they get a tax break for."

"When you do something charitable, do you brag about it?" he asked.

"No," I replied

"But you do mention it to someone, just to get a little credit for it, right?" he asked.

"No," I replied, a little offended and confused that he might even think that about me.

"Then why would you assume that other people, like those who have great wealth, would be so much different than yourself? Do you think money somehow causes a lack of concern for others?" he asked rhetorically. "Have you even thought about how much more the wealthy contribute and how they would be treated if they did brag about it or even share with others how much they give? These assumptions about the wealthy being greedy are just as destructive as some of the assumptions people have about truck drivers."

I could tell he did that to hit home with me, and it did. Being a bit defensive, I again tried to point out a flaw in his logic by using his words against him. I said, "So we shouldn't play God with others but it's okay when it comes to ourselves?"

"We don't have to play God, our very nature is divine," he replied. "The issue you are struggling with is the allowance of free will. When you impose your will on others, no matter how righteous you feel the reasoning, you do them a disservice."

"What about laws? Aren't they an imposition of will?" I asked, still searching for something that would trip him up.

"There are many laws that are, but laws should only be written to protect people from the imposition of the wills of others," he replied. "Otherwise, it's up to someone to determine what's best for everyone else, and you have to ask yourself who is infallible enough to do that. Before you even come up with an answer, though, remember that you probably won't get to choose."

"My head hurts. Can we stop?" I begged.

"Heady stuff, huh?" he said.

"Yeah, it's going to take a while to absorb. I don't even know if I will remember it all," I said.

"Yeah, maybe next time you should slow down a bit," he suggested.

"What? You're the one who barraged me with information," I complained and flashed him an irritated look.

"I simply answered your barrage of questions," he explained. "At times, it even felt as if I had to defend myself."

"Our realities are very different, aren't they," I asked sarcastically.

"Now you're getting it," he smiled. It failed to have its usual effect on me, though. I felt as if I had just spent a lot of time and energy trying to fit a square peg into a round hole. To have the round hole smile at me now was something I found less than appealing.

We sat in silence after that. I tried to focus on gratitude but my thoughts shifted to our conversation a lot. What he said had made sense but it sounded like it required a lot of faith in humanity. After a quite a while of reflection and then eating Matt's gourmet sandwiches, I got really tired so we pulled over for a nap.

Getting back on the road that afternoon, Matt wasted no time in returning to my training. "You know, I could really use a break right now," I protested halfheartedly.

"You just woke up from a nap," he smiled. "How much more of a break do you need?"

"This is really wearing on me," I pleaded. This pace was wearing my nerves thin. I felt like my mind was being stretched like saltwater taffy and he wasn't giving me enough time to adjust.

"I know, but this is a fun exercise and one you'll enjoy," he stated.

"I'm guessing I don't have a choice in the matter anyway," I complained. I guess whining comes naturally when you're doing any kind of training, and like most good trainers, Matt ignored my resistance and pressed on.

"Because our thoughts determine our realities, you have to start determining just what reality you wish to create," he began to explain.

"But I don't even know what reality I want to create," I countered.

"That's why you're going to do this exercise. You may not yet know exactly how you want to design your entire life right now, but you need to take a look at how you would design it if there were absolutely no limitations," he continued. "So I want you to spend some time every afternoon daydreaming about what you would do with a life without limitations. What if you could have, be, or experience anything you want in life? What would you want to have, or be, or experience? Most people never consider what their ideal life would look like because they don't see a way that it could be possible. In fact, merely to consider it causes them grief because in their hearts they know it's not possible."

"So you want to make me experience grief?" I asked, very puzzled at this statement.

"No, I want you to experience your desired reality," he replied.

"You just said it was impossible," I pointed out.

"No, I said that in their hearts they know it's not possible, and because they believe that it's not possible, it's not. Our predominant thoughts or beliefs create our reality. You will be creating a reality that has no limits and though you may not believe it yet, you need to start determining your preferences so that you can begin to get your thoughts in line with those preferences," he explained further. "These are things you won't be sharing with me, so don't hold back. Though I am a safe person to share such things with, in general you need to keep these desires to yourself. You are trying to accept a belief system that is held by very few, and it will generally be rejected and even scoffed at by others. Anything that discourages you from being able to adopt this belief system hinders your ability to create the limitless reality you desire."

"How am I going to accept such an enormous concept? Don't you see just how far outside the reality of most sane people this is?" I asked. I was beginning to grow tired of him being so nonchalant about all of this.

"You need to let go of the mentality of the masses if you want to live a life beyond their limitations," he stated very seriously. "The way you accept it is by repetition of the techniques that couple desired emotions with the desired reality, the same way you freed yourself from judgment. Why are you resisting so much now?"

"Because maybe I've tried already!" I snapped. "Maybe I've tried and failed and tried and failed and I don't want to get my hopes up one more time just to have another failure! You act like this is easy. It's not!"

"Wow, I didn't expect that," he said.

I thought maybe I had hurt his feelings, so I quickly apologized, "I'm sorry. This is just hard for me, that's all".

"No, it's not that," he explained. "I just wasn't expecting it that soon. You are really ready for this."

I slumped in my seat and sighed, "I can't do this right now. If you continue to speak in riddles, I'm out." I was wearing a look so somber that it was like a window to the sadness in my heart.

"I'm sorry. It's just that I've never had a student progress so quickly," he said. "What you're experiencing is your body's resistance to the change in your emotional state. The hypothalamus of the brain releases chemical peptides into the bloodstream based on our thoughts, which is how we experience emotion. They then attach themselves to various cells in our bodies. The cells in our bodies, in turn, become addicted to these peptides. Because our emotions are brought to us based on our thoughts, a change in thought patterns can throw off our physiology. This means that your thinking has already shifted enough that your body is resisting."

"Or maybe you just gave them a headache too. You went from speaking in riddles to speaking a different language. Please, make it stop," I pleaded, losing what little patience I had left.

"That's exactly what we're going to do," he replied. "You are going to just have to ride this out for today. You are going to honor the feelings you are experiencing. Oftentimes, when people feel bad, they assume that they are doing something wrong. This, my friend, is a sign you are doing something right. Feeling bad in this sense is a growing pain, and you are growing at a very fast pace. I am very proud of you. I am so glad I have comfort food on the menu for tonight. We're having stuffed pepper soup. I got the recipe off of the Internet. All the things you love about stuffed peppers in a thick and easy-to-consume soup." He then continued with a more gentle tone saying, "Your mind is about to beat you up for a while so you'll need all the comfort you can get."

"I'll be fine. Just give me a while," I stated. I then started seriously thinking. How the heck did he know what was going to go on in my head? I hated that he thought he knew more about me than I did. Who the heck was he anyway? He's just some damn guy running away from something, responsibility perhaps? He speaks in circles. This is a bunch of nonsense. He did free me from judgment. Was judgment holding me back? I did get something from that. I mean, I felt something, didn't I? This is BS. How is soup going to help me feel better? That's such a crock. That made me think of the fact that he's making it in the Crock-Pot and I smiled a little. Then my mind turned from Matt to me. So began the stoning of my mind with rocks made from truths about all of my failures. I would further describe the horrible details about just what it was like, but just how cruel one's own mind can be in this regard is so personal, you can only relate to your own. Driving a truck gives you a lot of time to think and I would have just as soon give that to someone else that day, but I was glad of two things: one, that my friend was by my side knowing what I was going through; and two, that he kept his big mouth shut.

Chapter 11

Clarity

"Morning," Matt said, handing me a cup of coffee. "Feeling better?" he asked.

"Yeah," I answered, finding it a bit strange. "Yeah, surprisingly I do feel a little better." I did feel better and I felt very humble in his presence now. Something changed, something within me. I took a sip of coffee before I could manage to meekly say, "Thank you."

He took a second to look at me because of the way I said it, and he could tell that I wasn't thanking him for the coffee. "You're welcome," he replied. "It was my pleasure, you know," he added with a smile.

"I know," I said. I somehow understood that all of what he had said was true and just how true it was. In this understanding, I realized that he was much more than merely a friend I had acquired who was passing on a little wisdom he had picked up along the way. In that moment I realized that this man was my guru, something I would no longer take for granted. I also realized just how important my responsibility was to pass along this information to someone else, because it was the only way I could repay him.

He wouldn't let me sit in awe of him for very long, though. "These beatings will be less severe and happen with less frequency as you continue to be habitual with your intent," he explained. "Soon enough they will be a thing of the past, but you must remember their lesson. What we need to do now is talk to your body."

"Talk to my body?" I questioned slowly.

"Yes. You need to explain to it that you understand that it likes you better the way you were, but that if it will just hang in there with you, it will like the new you so much better," he said as if this were perfectly logical.

I raised my head up just enough that I could look him in the eye and stared long enough to see that he wasn't kidding. "Do you have any idea how crazy that sounds?" I replied in a less-than-inspired tone, and then I felt a little ashamed at how quick I was to question his methods once again.

He started laughing so I thought maybe he was just kidding. "Yeah, it does sound crazy, right? But if it weren't important, I wouldn't have you do it."

I laughed too and noted, "Maybe it sounds crazy because it is crazy. Maybe you're just indoctrinating me into your insanity."

"Maybe people view the concept of living the life you love as pure insanity," he said, still grinning from ear to ear. "As I said before, we are trying to create a unity or harmony between the mind, body and soul.

Your mind and body are at odds now because of your recent shift in emotional state due to your training. You need to do this to try and bring them back into harmony." By the time he finished, he was back to being serious.

So I did try talking to my body, even though I felt somewhat silly. Then I commented, "I don't feel any different."

"No, you won't," he said. "Your thoughts control your emotions and you control your thoughts. Your body has the ability to send you messages, like to let you know that it needs food, and often will send you cravings for what it wants or needs. In this instance, it was craving the emotional peptides of your old thought patterns."

"Wait a minute, my thoughts weren't focused on what I want and appreciate all the time," I protested.

"No, but you cut it off from those peptides by changing your thought pattern, so it panicked a little. Just be glad you're not a drug addict. Those are some strong peptides. Imagine the conversations you'd have to have with your body for that," he said and then paused for effect. "Anyway, I'm sure it got a good enough fix for a while."

"Thanks again for being there for me while I was going through it, by the way," I said humbly. "And for the coffee," I added.

"Time for your journal," he said, handing me the list.

"No rest for the weary, huh?" I said, smiling a little.

"You were too sore to work out yesterday, but today we'll sweat yet again," he assured. "First journal, then general affirmations, expanding gratitude, lunch and figuring out what you really want, and, of course, solidifying the lessons."

"Yeah, woo-hoo," I said less than enthusiastically. "You did forget the best part, you know."

"Ah yes, dinner. I have all kinds of ideas," he assured me. I never understood how he knew exactly what I was talking about when I tried to be elusive with my questions.

So after updating my journal, we got back on the road and started what was to become our daily routine. I actually started looking forward to the regimen and was disappointed when it had to be broken up by the requirements of my job. I began to see how the more I focused on gratitude, the more grateful I became. The more grateful I became, the more happy (and humble) I found myself. The affirmations were not nearly as rewarding, but I got a kick out of doing them because I was getting really good at "acting," so to speak. I actually enjoyed getting into character for them. Some days, my journal would have something very profound, while others would be about the weather or something.

What I looked forward to the most, though, was designing my ideal life. It was also the one I had the most questions about, but I tried to keep them to myself. I finally broke down, though, and asked him, "You said that you flooded your thoughts with that of great wealth when you learned this principle. Would it have happened more easily or more quickly if you would have wanted less? I mean, is it easier for someone to create their reality the way they desire if their desires are more—I don't know—believable?"

His face lit up and his posture became more upright, "Ah, very astute observation," he said. "Just as there can be no limitation to that which you desire, there is no limitation for the universe to grant that which you desire. In fact, it is a very easy and natural process."

I tried to hide my excitement about this knowledge, but I couldn't quite contain my smile. No one had ever told me I could have anything I want before. "So, if I want a million dollars by the end of the week?" I asked.

He laughed. "They always ask the million dollar question," he said. "I don't know what it is about that number, but it's never a billion or ten million. Every student I have throws out the hypothetical million dollar question. I get a kick out of it every time."

His mood may have been brightened by my question, but mine had been dampened by his response. "I'm happy you find this so entertaining, but what's the answer?"

"The universe responds in kind to the vibrations your thoughts resonate at. This means that in order for you to get a million dollars, you must believe you are worth a million dollars. Do you believe you are worth a million dollars?" he asked.

I felt disappointed at that. "I feel I am as worthy as anyone else," I replied.

"I didn't ask you if you felt worthy. I asked you if you felt you are worth a million dollars," he clarified.

"No, I am not worth a million dollars and I have a recent bank statement that can prove it," I said, a little peeved because it was obvious.

"If you don't believe it, the universe won't either," he explained. "Whatever you believe becomes your reality. That is why we are working so hard to expand your beliefs."

"So I should start with something small and work my way up maybe?" I suggested.

"You certainly can do it that way. There is a school of thought that considers that to be the best method. The principle behind it is that you shift your way of thinking incrementally so that it doesn't go beyond your belief system," he explained unenthusiastically. "But if you're not expanding your consciousness, you will never experience bliss in this lifetime. It will probably take you much more than a week to expand your consciousness enough to include being a millionaire, but your limitations are self-created. They are based on your reaction to input. You surmised, based on what you have experienced, that it is very difficult to be a millionaire and it is certainly not something that happens in a week. This was reactionary thinking and I am helping you to become a visionary thinker. Becoming a visionary requires you to habitually focus on a desired reality, not your current one."

"So it's a matter of expanding your consciousness to accommodate your desires, rather than diluting your desires to accommodate your belief system," I summarized.

"Yeah, that's a good way to put it," he said. "Do you mind if I use that?"

"Of course not," I replied. In the beginning of our relationship, I had expected him to have all the answers and be without flaw, but as I was finding the perfection and beauty in everything, I realized that my expectations had shifted and that, in and of itself, was an expansion of consciousness.

I drifted back into thoughts of what my ideal life would look like. There was one thing that was very apparent to me when I let go of limitations, and that was that my job was no longer a fit. I loved traveling but with the schedule I had, I didn't get any time to enjoy it, and what was the point of traveling if I didn't have a traveling companion? Actually, I needed a companion regardless. Spending time with Matt, someone who mentally challenged me, I could no longer ignore the fact that I was very lonely. Also, my heart kept directing my mind toward my piano player. She was so amazing. I knew I wasn't supposed to focus on a specific person but I wondered if I could use her as a guideline. I thought about writing her, I mean my future girlfriend, love letters. He had mentioned something about using creativity on that answer website. His answer seemed really dry though. It was like reading an instruction manual. I always tried to keep my answers more personal so that they would seem more interesting to the reader. In fact, I really enjoyed writing. Before I went to college, I took an aptitude test and it required that I give them two areas of interest. My areas of interest were mechanical engineering and writing. It was determined that although I would make a great mechanical engineer, I would probably be a failure as a writer. Since I was more interested in mechanical engineering anyway, I didn't protest the results, but I wondered how they came to that conclusion about my being a writer, having read little to none of my work. Ultimately, it was all for naught, though, because I couldn't stay motivated enough to finish school and eventually dropped out.

I also had to take a look at the lifestyle I wanted. Matt was right about my being resentful toward those who had money. I was jealous. I thought myself to be better than them because if I had the money I would spend it differently. When I examined myself in this regard, I found myself to be more arrogant than I was accusing them of being. When I took a look at it all from a higher perspective and removed judgment, I discovered that I did want to be wealthy, at least wealthy enough to support my other desires. I even looked forward to the day that I could say that without some degree of shame. Matt had said that when we express the divine within by following our desires, we live life in abundance in all aspects of life. I understood that for me to fight against this desire because of my own judgment would prove detrimental to not only me but others as well. If I denied my desires I would not be as happy, and therefore not as useful to others. All of this was starting to sink in and again, I was humbled by it.

After about a week of this routine, I could see a notable improvement in my reaction to things that used to stress me out. Matt had pointed out how now that I was giving my life direction, things would start happening, but I wouldn't be able to recognize how until everything came together. This meant that I could have been getting aggravated about the very thing that was bringing me closer to my desires. That seemed to help, though I found that trying to figure out how to do it was a futile endeavor. My whole world was changing fast, especially in terms of my peace of mind.

As I kept answering questions on the answer website, I found my answers were becoming too long for the parameters of the site. I was starting to understand why Matt's answer seemed so dry – it was highly concentrated. There were so many people who needed the answers Matt had given me. It was then that I decided not only what I wanted to do but how I was going to repay my friend. I have the heart of a writer and no aptitude test can tell me otherwise. That test hadn't really discouraged me that much, though, because I had already given up on that dream before I took it. I was just hoping that maybe the test would show that I had promise. No, I had already bought into the idea—as so many do with their dream jobs—that only the best of the best make a good living at it and the chances of me being the best of the best were so slim that it was illogical to even try. Even the idea of writing entire books seemed too daunting a task to attempt. But now I was going to give up all of my expectations, make my declaration, and leave the rest to the universe.

Chapter 12

Saying Goodbye

"I know what it is that I want to do," I proclaimed.

He smiled and said, "Good. Now keep it to yourself."

"But I want to share it with you. I know you said that I need to protect myself from discouragement, but I need to share it with someone because I'm so excited about it and you said yourself that you are safe," I stated, making my case.

"You still have their voices in your head," he said.

"I don't think I'm as crazy as you may think," I said, wearing a look of confusion.

"How many times have you said you were going to do something in life and were all excited about it, telling all who would listen, only for it never to come to fruition?" he asked.

"I don't know, a few at least," I answered.

"Until it's been long enough for your body to stop resisting, it will tell you that this is just one more of

189

those times, and that to share it with someone else would just allow them to add shame and embarrassment to the list," he explained. "You can't afford to give your body ammunition right now."

"Oh," I said, reflecting on what he said. "That makes sense." He could see the expression of disappointment I was wearing.

"It is wonderful that you now know what direction you want to go, though, because I want to share with you a very fun and effective technique," he said excitedly. "It's my favorite. It's called the interview technique. Basically, you envision yourself being interviewed by someone who is interested in what you do. You picture them asking questions like, 'How did you get started? What made you decide to do what you do? Who were your greatest influences?' Stuff like that."

"That sounds kinda fun," I said.

"It is fun," he said. "I did it about once a week when I started. Do it much more than that and it can get a little boring. It also helps to achieve that feeling of sharing your dreams with others without actually doing it."

"Okay, cool. I'm going to try that," I said excitedly. And I did, along with the rest of my routine for another week. In addition to the general affirmations he had me do, he had me silently do ones that were specifically related to my desires. Since he didn't let me tell him what my desires were, I had to make the affirmations up myself. He said that they work better when you personalize them anyway. I wouldn't say that anything revolutionary happened during that time. I really enjoyed his company and his food, though. It was then that he dropped the bomb on me.

"We're having a feast tonight," he said.

"We usually do," I said. "Must be really special if you're announcing it, though. What's up?"

"It's our last night together so I thought I'd make something really special," he proclaimed.

"Last night together?" I repeated questioningly. "You mean you're leaving?"

"Yeah, it's time to move on, you know, find my next victim and all," he said.

I looked into his eyes to see if he was serious. He was. "But I thought…," I said and the words just kind of hung there. "But…" I shook my head a little in confusion, trying to come up with the words to say.

"You thought I would hold your hand all the way?" he asked rhetorically but very gently. "I've taught you all you need to know to get where you want to go, but I can't take you there."

"You said you could," I said meekly, not wanting to give him up yet, but still knowing what he meant. This was so unexpected. I thought gurus stuck around until the student becomes a master. I was far from being a master.

"No. I said I could get you where you want to go. I didn't say I would take you there. We all have to do our own homework in life and you now understand exactly what that entails," he explained. "You now know how to get anywhere you want to go in life, how to get anything you want in life, how to be anything you want and how to experience anything you want. In doing those things, you will express your true nature. I have been your guide thus far, but it is time for you to find your inner guide. It is time for it to take over. For me to stick around would only hinder your growth. I have taught you how to be intentional habitually. I can plant the seed and water it, but I cannot make the tree within grow."

"But I don't want an inner guide, I want you," I protested somewhat jokingly.

He smiled and looked at me for a minute. "You're going to do great things," he said.

"But you haven't even told me how the universe will bring about my desired reality," I pleaded. "How will I know what to do? How will I know if I'm doing the right thing? How do I?…"

He stopped me by bringing his finger to his lips. That was all it took, because I was too distraught to argue. "First, everything is fluent with the universe. Unlike the effort required for expanding your consciousness, the effort required to create your desired reality will seem more like fun. Secondly, if you ignore the first nudge from the universe, it will repeat itself, so if things come up more than once, pay attention. Thirdly, relax. Once you are intentional with your thoughts, your desired reality will happen. It then becomes meant to be."

Even though I wanted to make more of an issue out of what he said, I found myself understanding that this wasn't about that. This was about me being on my own again, and not just on my spiritual path. I wanted to quickly change the subject, though, so I wouldn't seem as saddened as I was, so I somberly asked, "What are we feasting on?"

"Enlightenment stew," he replied with a grin. "So you'll never eat stew again without thinking of me."

"If you put that onion in my mouth again, you won't have any teeth to eat the stew with," I joked.

"You're such a baby. I'm amazed I was able to get your thumb out of your mouth long enough to teach you anything," he kidded back. And so it went until we went to sleep. I had decided to hold my disappointment until he was gone and enjoy his company and cuisine while he was still here.

I didn't get to say goodbye to him the next morning. He had done it again. He snuck by me while I was sleeping. He left a note giving me his e-mail address and requested that I keep in touch. He said that he was going to continue reading my answers on that site to be certain I was on track and if I had any more questions just to email him. I couldn't believe he just left like that. I thought I was at least going to drop him off somewhere, maybe a bus station or something. I didn't even get to drink a final cup of coffee with him.

And so began my loneliness. In the small amount of time that he was with me, I had forgotten what eating alone in a restaurant felt like. I had forgotten what solitude felt like. I had forgotten what it was like to witness something funny or beautiful and not to be able to turn to someone and share it with them. I honored those feelings, all right. I let them envelop me as I drowned in a sea of loneliness and self-pity. For almost three days I indulged in those feelings. But on the third day, I got my focus back once again. I was going to help people. I was going to share with others what Matt had given to me. I was going to succeed in creating my life to match my vision of it.

In the coming months, I made my declarations to the universe very clear. I even started writing my book, though I wasn't sure exactly where I was going with it, and I found myself becoming distracted by the answer website. I enjoyed it so much that I would answer questions for hours on end and then I would scold myself for not working more on my book. Matt had said that everything I have to do to achieve my goals would be enjoyable and to trust the universe, but this was clearly a distraction. I even considered that maybe I was going to somehow get paid to answer people's questions because I enjoyed it so much, but quickly dismissed that idea as I could not see how that could be possible.

As it turned out, answering the questions on that website helped me clarify my ideas for the book. It helped me understand just what people were struggling with and how best to address the issues in relation to my new perspective. In this fashion, the book also served to solidify the lessons of my guru.

In fact, many things were falling into place for me. About a year after my Matt and I parted ways, I was just finishing writing my novel. That's when I met Alexandra. That's right, my crush introduced herself to me. I was sitting in a café, doing a general editing of my first draft, when she came to my table and sat down. She said that she believed everything happens for a reason and seeing me three times, in three different parts of the country had to mean something. I remember being so excited because it meant that not only had she noticed me at the restaurant, but she had seen me in a suit. I also remember how strange it was that chatting with her came so easily. I was actually very confident. Maybe it was due to the fact that her saying how everything happens for a reason spurred my going into details about it, which I had become quite passionate about. She wasn't all that receptive to a lot of what I had to say, and I took it quite personally. She wasn't meeting the expectations of what I thought she'd be like and, because of that, I decided that the universe was letting me know that it was better suited to play matchmaker, so I resolved to just be friends with her.

We spoke on the phone every day, though. Since we both had jobs that required travel, it was nice to no longer be alone on the road. We tried to synchronize our schedules so that we could hang out at least once a week, and though my dispatcher gave me trouble by continually reminding me that he was not my travel agent, it worked out rather well. In fact, we are currently engaged to be married. Apparently, I'm not very good at interpreting the universe, but it seems to compensate somehow for this.

As far as being wealthy goes, I no longer care about it. I can't wait until I have enough money to travel the country with Alexandra instead of merely arranging brief encounters, but I feel so abundant already that I know the money will be there in the amount necessary for my happiness.

Sometimes, I wonder what my life would look like if I hadn't met that oddly dressed man at the truck stop, telling me he could get me where I want to go. I don't think I could ever again live like I was before I met him. Once someone shows you how good life can be and how to make it so, you can never go back. I miss him being around sometimes, but I still keep in contact with him via e-mail and I will see him again at the wedding, as he's agreed to be the best man. He also said he'd come around now and again after I bear fruit, as he put it, just as he does with Robert.

I know I'll see Matt again soon because everything I do in life now is an expression of who I truly am. I no longer allow my reality to be determined by my reaction to other people, circumstances or events. I am quickly becoming a vibrational match to my desired reality and I know it won't be long before it's realized. I will keep the promises I made to my guru, though. I will never hitchhike across the country in pajamas, led by the universe to help desperate souls. But I will make damn sure that the message of the man who does, doesn't die with me.